Our Side of the River:
Volume Two
The Place We Call Home

Written by

The Students of Benton Harbor Area Schools

2021

Our Side of the River Volume 2: The Place We Call Home
Benton Harbor Area Schools

ISBN: 978-1-387-33124-6

Copyright © 2021 by SPI First Printing

All rights reserved. This book or any portion thereof may not be reproduced or used in any manner whatsoever without the express written permission of the publisher except for the use of brief quotations in a book review or scholarly journal

Benton Harbor Area Schools Educators

Ms. Michele Vogt-Schuller, Summer School Administrator
Ms. Lesa Hamilton, English Teacher, BHHS
Mr. Ian Mosher, English Teacher, BHAS
Ms. Natalie Logan, English Teacher, BHHS
Ms. JanElla Schnepp, Reading Interventionist, BHAS
Ms. Regina Strother, English Teacher, BHAS
Mr. Jason Wolf, English Teacher, BHHS

Photos unless otherwise specified, provided by:

The Benton Harbor History Project, Summer 2021

SPI Educator and Publication Coach

Jennifer DeCerff

The Student Press Initiative (SPI)
Center for the Professional Education of Teachers

Director and Founder, Dr. Ruth Vinz
Center Director, Dr. Roberta Lenger Kang
Initiatives Director, Dr. Cristina Compton
SPI Founding Director, Dr. Erick Gordon
Cover Design, Kapo Amos Ng
Editorial Team, Natalie Davis-Porada and Lindi Shepard

Center for the Professional Education of Teachers
Teachers College, Columbia University
525 West 120th Street
New York, NY 10027

www.cpet.tc.columbia.edu

Contents

Acknowledgements   8
Foreword   10
Introduction   12

Chapter One: Our Town, Our School

Teona Bell	14
Denim Collins	15
Monteonna Duckett	16
Elisha Guidry	17
Trinity Henry	18
Ke'Lasha Mays	19
Classie Newbern	20
Classie Newbern	21
Aubrey Watters	23
Star Williams	24

Chapter Two: In This Place

Mylon Bowman	26
C'myah Boyd	28
Gregory Charles Jones	29
Margaret Pratt	30
Asia Tillman	31
Christine Gonzalez-Stubbs	32

Chapter Three: Coming From Where I'm From

Teona Bell	34
C'myah Boyd	35
Kenyatta Cooper	36
Dominik Henderson	37
Paul Hicks III	38
Ka'Veona Huddleston	38
Gregory Charles Jones	39

Kamerion Killman	40
Antonio Mendoza	41
Char'Naja Moody	42
Jo'Shaun Porter	42
Margaret Pratt	43
Avantae Ross	44
Asia Tillman	44
Tiania Tyson	45
Star Williams	46

Chapter Four: Student Reflections

Teona Bell	48
Jonairo Chatman	49
Kenyatta Cooper	50
Monteonna Duckett	50
Ar'Janiya Gray	51
Paul Hicks III	52
Danny Jennings	53
Quentin Young-McCutchen	54
Antonio Mendoza	55
Antonito Mendoza	56
Char'Naja Moody	56
Classie Newbern	57
Jo'Shawn Palmer	58
Avontae Ross	59
Deshawn Swanson	59
Kamerion Tillman	60
Tiania Tyson	60
Tiania Tyson	61
Aubrey Watters	63
Javion Williams	63
Star Williams	64

Chapter Five: Nature Writings

Teona Bell	67
Emaria Campbell	68
Emaria Campbell	69
Kenyatta Cooper	70
Janaha Ewing	70
Paul Hicks III	71
Ka'Veona Huddleston	72
Danny Jennings	73
Antonio Mendoza	74
Char'Naja Moody	75
Classie Newbern	76
Jo'Shaun Palmer	77
Avontae Ross	78
Kamerion Tillman	79
Tiania Tyson	80
Star Williams	81

Chapter 6: Essays of Place by 11th and 12th Grade Writers

Jakia Boatner	85
Denarion Evans	92
Sean Sargeant	100
Tyra Williams	107

Chapter Seven: Believing, Hoping and Dreaming

Teona Bell	116
C'myah Boyd	118
C'myah Boyd	119
Emaria Campbell	120
Christine Gonzalez-Stubbs	121
Dominik Henderson	121
Gregory Charles Jones	122

Gregory Charles Jones	123
Antonio Mendoza	124
Char'Naja Moody	124
Jo'Shaun Palmer	125
Margaret Pratt	126
Margaret Pratt	126
Avontae Ross	128
Deshawn Swanson	128
Asia Tillman	129
Asia Tillman	130
Tiania Tyson	131
Javion Williams	131
Star Williams	132

Chapter Eight: Thinking in Metaphor

Ta'Nae Allen	134
Marlon Bowman	135
Aniya Daniels	136
Jordan Henry	136
Paul Hicks III	137
Danny Jennings	138
Alexis Kirkland	139
Damarion Lewis	140
Tyler Meeks	141
Antonio Mendoza	142
Char'Naja Moody	143
Classie Newbern	144
Davis Powell	145
Kentrell Pullian	146
Avontae Ross	147
Kamerion Tillman	148
Tiania Tyson	149
Synesha Ware	150
Jerome White Jr.	151
Kobe White	152

Star Williams	153
Damarious Woods	154

Chapter Nine: Orange and Black

Ta'nae Allen	156
Teonna Bell	157
Kyle Booth	157
Marlon Bowman	157
Mylon Bowman	158
Emaria Campbell	158
Kenyatta Cooper	159
Keewayn Fleming	159
William Fryson	160
Jordan Henry	161
Danny Jennings	161
Koreyanna Jones-Vison	161
Arlandrea Lamb	162
Jakira McClinton	163
Tyler Meeks	163
Classie Newbern	164
Davis Powell	164
Kentrell Pullian	164
Jamarious Sanders	165
Toney Walker	166
Synesha Ware	166
Kobe White	167
Damarious Woods	167

Acknowledgements

This book was generously funded by a grant from the Benton Harbor Education Foundation (BHEF) and the Benton Harbor Area Schools (BHAS) learning community who enthusiastically supported this project. Thank you, Ryan Goble, Ed.D., and Michele Vogt-Schuller for initiating this book project during the Covid-19 pandemic, for your leadership, guidance and vision for amplifying student voice through writing for publication.

With special thanks to…

The BHEF and the Whirlpool Corporation's support. Our deep appreciation goes to the leadership of Alloyd P. Blackmon and the support of the BHEF team in making this project a possibility.

The Benton Harbor Area Schools leadership & staff including Dr. André Townsel, Dr. Lawanna Shelton, Dr. Kyle Krol, Mark Miller, Tracy Davis, Elizabeth Gayle, Scott Johnson and the entire Central Office Team as well as the Board of Education of Benton Harbor Area Schools for supporting this project.

The high school and middle school BHAS educators who participated in our kickoff event and have continued on the journey of student publication by championing writing in their classrooms. Thank you, Lesa Hamilton, Natalie Logan, Ian Mosher, JanElla Schnepp, Regina Strother, Michele Vogt-Shuller and Jason Wolf.

The leadership at the Center for the Professional Education of Teachers (CPET) Dr. Ruth Vinz and Dr. Roberta Lenger Kang at Teachers College, Columbia University in New York City. To Student Press Initiative (SPI) coaches, Dr. Cristina Romeo Compton and Jen DeCerff, who worked with the project from launch to publication.

Thank you to singer, actress, dancer, and choreographer, Ms. Niki Haris, for writing the foreword and endorsing this book project. Calling Benton Harbor her hometown, her words challenge us all to see the dreams and realities of Benton Harbor Areas Schools' young authors.

Most of all, it is the student writers who we thank for their courage in sharing their words and images with us, for persevering in their writing, living life, and for speaking their truth in the time of Covid.

Foreword

"Hold High Our Shields of Orange and Black
We See Our Banners Proudly Waving,
Fight, Fight Until the Last
We're with You BHHS!"

I sang those words weekly as a Benton Harbor High School cheerleader. For 4 years in the late 1970's, that stanza was ingrained in my consciousness. That cadence helped me stand tall and remember to aspire to great heights as I stood on the shoulders of those who had gone before me, all the while filling me with inspiration for a brighter future.

Words can do that. Words allow us to go places in our minds and dream of the unknown. Words can be "Shields" and act as "Banners" we proudly wave.

I have watched my small Midwest town of Benton Harbor (technically a TWIN CITY) suffer economically and continue to be marginalized. The OTHER "TWIN " seems to ALWAYS have the "new shoes" while my "TWIN" wears hand-me-downs on it's BEST days! I have wondered if the children growing up there NOW still hold their "Shields" high. Did they still know the power within them? Did they know their own "Words" could carry them to unknown places even while navigating decaying corridors?

After reading excerpts from the student writings gathered in this book, I can only respond with a resounding YES!!!!!
It fills me with gratitude and optimism that these young writers have chosen to tell their stories and share their poems. Most importantly, they are courageous enough to tell their truths!!

Martin Luther, the German priest and author said, "If you want to change the world, pick up a pen and write…" (cont'd)

I am under no delusions that these writings will change the world, but I do know these writers will be forever changed for having put pen to paper.
English author, Neil Gaiman is quoted as saying, "A Book is a 'Dream' you hold in your hands..."
You now hold these young writers 'Dreams' in your hands. As you turn the pages, let each word be a gentle touch to wake Us all from our slumber...

Enjoy..... Niki Haris

Niki Haris, a multi-talented singer, dancer, actress and choreographer, is the daughter of GRAMMY Award-nominated jazz pianist Gene Harris. Best known as "The Big Voice" behind Madonna for over 18 years, she appeared alongside her in the movie *Truth or Dare*. She has worked with Jazz greats like Stanley Turrentine, Joe Sample and the Jazz Crusaders, recorded with greats from Ray Charles to Mick Jagger and from Whitney Houston to Sheryl Crow. Ms. Haris has played from Carnegie Hall to Wembley Stadium.

She was called to sing for the inauguration of President Barack Obama, performing with will.iam., and has continued to share her musical gifts by supporting AIDS Research, The Human Rights Campaign (HRC), as well as Camp Harmony, benefiting the lives of inner city children. Her support of Music in the Classroom, and "RAAD," (Rockers Against Drunk Driving) keeps her busy and committed to their success. Currently, Niki Haris remains an international pop and jazz performer, as well as being a dedicated mother to her high school daughter, Jordan.

Introduction

Benton Harbor, Summer 2021

After spending much of the school year at home, students returned to Benton Harbor High School in the summer of 2021. Many students and teachers had struggled with how so much of what they had known about school had abruptly changed. Summer School at Benton Harbor Area Schools provided teachers and students the opportunity to come together in smaller groups to create intimate learning communities. It is out of these communities at Benton Harbor High School and Fair Plain Middle School that this book emerged, led by the efforts of Jason Wolf, Ian Mosher, Lesa Hamilton, Natalie Logan, Jenella Schepp and Regina Strothers and their students.

I took up the job of summer school administrator for the high school, and everything went smoothly. Thanks to our staff of student advocates, Maurice Burton, Kenya Ellis, and Mary Singer, the things that a school administrator might have to worry about during school essentially disappeared. I could often walk through the halls and visit classrooms and see small groups of students and teachers working together. In this collaborative, intentional school community, both at the high school and middle school, a book about the place of Benton Harbor emerged.

I was fortunate to work with some of Mr. Wolf's students during their writing process, and what I learned from these students was their Benton Harbor; their childhood experiences, jobs, participation in sports, their friendships, what they do for fun. It's all the normal stuff that teenagers do: ride around in cars, play video games, and hang out with friends.

In this second volume, there are also stories of great loss—friends move or pass away. Underneath these stories, poems and short writings lie an awareness that Benton Harbor is a special place; one of great beauty and power, but also danger, the biggest of which is there are not enough places to go, and that many people in this town get stuck. In a conversation with Tyra Williams, I asked her if she knew why the men she wrote about walk around Benton Harbor, and she answered, "They're not ready."

It's my hope that the student authors of this book, and all of our BHAS students, become ready to enter into the world. As adults, community members, educators—well, all of us—it's our job to help them get ready for what comes next. This publication is a way to get their stories out there, a way to participate in the world outside of Benton Harbor.

It has been my deep honor to help foster this incredible book with the students and adults in Benton Harbor Area Schools and experience returning to face to face learning this summer. As you read, I hope you will experience a sense of the place that is Benton Harbor.

Michele Vogt-Schuller
Summer School Administrator
Benton Harbor High School

Chapter One
Our Town, Our School

Benton Harbor School Building
By Teona Bell (Grade 12)

I started with positivity,
I was a good thing, but
Good things can turn bad.
Positives turned into negatives.
Still, I am something you won't forget.
I provide for my district;
A lot of children look up to me.

Orange & black—
Colors of Halloween—
A scary holiday.
Screaming children,
Happy children,
I hold a mixture,
But I can't paint a perfect picture,
That is my truth.

I am not the best anymore,
But I still hold purpose.
I have children to care for & they are worth it.
Even though I seem tired,
I still remain home of the Tigers;
I am The Benton Harbor High School Building.

What Does Benton Harbor Mean To Me?
By Denim Collins (Grade 7)

Well it's not the fanciest place. In fact, if you walk around the sidewalk is broken and worn over by grass. A lot of people would ask me what does the way a place looks like have to do with anything? Usually I would have said nothing, but it does. It changes how comfortable you are, and your surroundings represent the people that live there. Don't get me wrong, I love my city. It's where I'm coming up. But what does it mean to me is the question. It means being able to say I love my city through thick and thin, even when it's at its worst. So I think it means a lot.

Denim Collins is a student at FPMS. He is a brilliant and promising child. He is academically outstanding and will for SURE graduate at the very least a year before his peers and he is remarkable.

Benton Harbor
By Monteonna Duckett (Grade 7)

I don't like Benton Harbor.
Benton Harbor is nasty and very trashy. Benton Harbor could be fixed.
We should change the stores
And change the doors.
A door to freedom
A door to happiness
A door to no killing
Then we could make it better! But would it even matter?
It's not about that change,
It's about the people
And how they treat our town.
Make our town better
Make it matter
This is our town
Our home!

My Home
By Elisha Guidry (Grade 7)

Hi my name is Elisha Guidry. I'm 12 years old, born September 1. Birthday on the way. I was born and raised in Benton Harbor. Benton Harbor has always been my home since I was born. So many nice people live here, and it just brings me happiness. Sometimes I wish that I moved but I can't. All my family and friends are here, and if I leave I will have nothing but my Mom and siblings. People think that Benton Harbor is a messed up and crazy town, but in reality Benton Harbor is filled with happiness and joy.

Even though Benton Harbor ain't a big city it's the thought that counts cause most big cities have no love or happiness. It's just a big city to them. I lost so many people this 2020, but my great grandma before she passed said, "When I die I want you to make sure that you won't cry and be sad." Those are the last words I heard from her before she passed. Benton Harbor is a town where we say hi and bye and how are you and see you next week things like that.

It's like a movie when you see how Benton Harbor was made. If you don't know, Benton Harbor used to be called Brunson Harbor, started by the name Eleazer Morton and two other men. There is so much history in this town. My school year in Benton Harbor so far is going good, lots of people being nice…. *SOMETIMES* when they want to. I came from a public school that I've been to for 6 years, and even got bullied to a school where most parents don't take their kids. Things change. I planned on staying at that school until I graduated but anyway Benton Harbor will always be a part of my heart and I hope it will be a part of yours. Things in this town will forever last, and there are many more things to come in this town.

I Am Benton Harbor High School 12
By Trinity Henry (Grade 12)

I'm Benton Harbor High School,
And we do a lot of big things here.
We live large.

As the building of
Benton Harbor High School,
I have a long history…

People know us for our
Tiger's Basketball Team…

We are CHAMPIONS!

I'm the best high school,
And others love me, and
I love you.

Untitled
By Ke'Lasha Mays (Grade 7)

My favorite places in Benton Harbor are my house and the Boys & Girls Club because they're fun places to be. My home is nice and comfortable. It smells like air-freshener. My Mom, sister, and brother are there with me. I can walk to a park and store, but I cannot walk to school. I can watch tv, be on my phone, and be with my mom and my siblings. The Boys and Girls Club is where I go to see my friends and have fun with my friends. My house and the Boys and Girls Club are my favorite places to be.

Ke'Lasha Mays is a student at FPMS and is in the 7th grade. In her free time she goes to the Boys and Girls Club to have fun with her friends and plays basketball. She lives in Benton Harbor.

I Believe
By Classie Newbern (Grade 12)

I believe
Living in Benton Harbor wouldn't be so
Hard,
But some
People don't even know you or
Your story,
They just judge based on the place
You stay.

Nobody knows us, but yet they have so
Much to say, just 'cause they feel we are
Worthless,
Other than meaningful, like any other
City like Berrien Springs or St. Joseph.

I'm not from Benton Harbor, but this is
My home that I've been living in and I
Cherish it.

I promise, before it's all said and done,
The world will appreciate Benton Harbor,
Just as much as I do,
Because I believe we can make this city
Whole again and have the same
Respect as any other city.

Benton Harbor High School Building
By Classie Newbern (Grade 12)

Hello, there...

Special greetings from the building of Benton Harbor High School.
I was born/built in 1872, which was the first location of Central School.
In 1872, I had all grades inside my stomach,
From elementary school to high school kids.
Today I am 147 years old, and feel every bit of it.

I have seen so many kids work so hard coming to me everyday,
To make sure they get the education that they need.
At times, I feel like I am everyone's grandma,
Because I have watched little kids grow up to be so big and successful in life,
Which has been truly a joy to witness.

But over the years, it hasn't been easy for me.
I have had a lot of accomplishments in my life,
But the bad has been overweighing the good lately.

The bad has been people that never even met me,
But disliked me and wanted to
Shut me down for good, if that happened, I would die...
Yet, as of right now, in the year 2020, I am still alive and standing,
Due to new people running me and trying to
Keep me open for the kids.

Money has always been the problem to keep me around.
It takes alot to keep me open.
Overall, I'm very thankful for having people that I had help me
Stay open.
I try to stay open for the people who I love and cherish,
So I can keep the kids of the future, whose
Parents and grandparents came to me for an education in the past,
Educated and keep the Tiger legacy going for generations to come...

I am The Benton Harbor High School Building, and I plan on sticking around.

Benton Harbor
by Aubrey Watters (Grade 7)

Benton Harbor is a Rose.
It blooms with Joy.
We are Tigers.
We fight for what's Right.

Benton Harbor is Danger.
Too many kids are killed over Foolishness. Too much Hate
Given by people you don't even Know.

People get Hurt
Every day of the Week.
People kidnap kids and molest Them Until they get what they
think is Right.

Benton Harbor can be millions of Things If violence wasn't the
Answer.
Stop the violence in Benton Harbor… and anywhere else.

I The Benton Harbor High School Building
By Star Williams (Grade 12)

I am an old building,
Standing many bricks tall,
Full of gifted students,
Trophies and all.

When many step feet step in time within my halls,
I feel that Tiger Beat;
I bleed orange and black.

When people hear about me,
They automatically think negatively,
But I remain to stand many bricks tall,
Because I'm not ashamed of me.

Chapter Two
In This Place

In This Place Is Happiness
By Mylon Bowman (Grade 12)

What Happiness is to me is love, the feeling of my spirit with joy, and refreshing my mind and soul. I need to free my soul and mind from issues to be happy. Happiness is the long walk in the warm weather of the earth, seeing the thick white clouds, blue skies, and bright, yellow, sunny sunshine above me, with its scorching warm heat.

What happiness is to me is crowds of others, smiling, social and full of positive talk. Talk that speaks of encouragement, truth, and love. Smiles that are full of joy, relief, and courage. Social activity with friends and family.

What happiness is to me is sports, the sore muscles, hard practice, the taste of salty sweat dripping down from my steaming, and warm forehead of the body. It is the sound of the coach yelling, yelling words of hard work and encouragement, with the high pitched stretched sound of the whistle coming from the blow of the coaches mouth and the feeling of the rubbery rough football gliding through the air. It's the smell of the fresh-cut, green grass mixing with the brown soil of dirt and the sight of teammates working hard and not giving up.

What happiness is to me is puppies, fluffy thick soft fur, the feeling of the puppies wet tongue of love, the sight of the puppies lovable happy smile, the speeding of the wagging tail, feeling of the spirit of love from the puppies, the sight of the tiny size, and the sound of the high pitched bark of the puppies feelings of the excitement of the puppies.

What happiness is to me in this place is relaxing music and the soothing encouraging words of love. Happiness is the joyful feeling of thoughts running through your head of goodness. It is the love and precious feeling of peace to the soul of a loving message of information that relieves the soul.

In This Place
By C'myah Boyd (Grade 12)

In this place I am alone.
In this place it is dark.

In this place it's just me,
Stuck in my own thoughts.

Always inside of my head,
Thoughts wandering, trying
To escape such a dark place.

In this place, I'm always
Thinking about the bad...I'm
Ready to think about the good.

It's time to escape…

In this place I am not ok.

But once I am out
Of this place,
I will be okay.

In this place I will get over whatever I need.

In this place I will be okay.

In This Place
By Gregory Charles Jones (Grade 12)

In this place, Benton Harbor, Michigan,
Where many untold secrets lie.
A tree waits to blossom;
Where negativity goes to die.

In this place, Benton Harbor, Michigan,
A town split by dark and light.
Some believe in this place,
While others just fight.

In this place, Benton Harbor, Michigan,
Where memories form.
The weather is like our emotions.
Sometimes cold, sometimes warm.

In this place, Benton Harbor, Michigan,
It has an ugly cover for its book.
There's so many wondrous things inside,
You just have to look.

In This Place
By Margaret (Big Margo) Pratt (Grade 12)

In this place I feel alone…
I'm ashamed, almost.
I feel like a failure.
I'm being the best
I can be,
But I'm being pressured to be something
I'm not.

I question myself wondering if I've accomplished
Enough,
If I'm where I need to be.

How can I be in a place
Where I can't be me.
I'm not selfish.
I'm human.
No more pressure.
I am me, and
That's all that I should be.

In This Place
By Asia Tillman (Grade 12)

In this place there is darkness,
Such confusion and hurt.
Decisions Decisions Decisions
How should I feel today?

It's cold here, but I still need
To find her.

So lost and full
Of deep emotion and betrayal.
Where are you in this place?

In this place I'm alone.
Self, "Please come and find me."

I have made friends with my demons.

In This Place
By Christine Gonzalez-Stubbs (Grade 12)

In this place I call my room,
When feeling down,
I don't like to be around people
When I'm mad.
It's not a good thing.
I don't want nobody to be thinking
Bad energy,
So I go away.

I hope for one day
I be what I wanna be in life.
It's hard right now, but
I'm not giving up.
I wanna make my family and friends
Proud.

My time is going to come.
I'm just learning things still,
But I'm going to be everything
I put my mind to.

Chapter Three
Coming From Where I'm From

I'm Tired Of
By Teona Bell (Grade 12)

I am tired of waking up early in the morning.
It is very irritating fighting my sleep to stay awake.
I am tired of setting many alarms,
Just to wake up in time, never getting enough sleep.

I am tired of dealing with Covid.
I do not like the masks.
I do not like how everything has changed.
I do not like the fact that hospitals can't have visitors.

I am tired of sharing rooms with my sisters.
I am tired of not having my own space.
I am tired of having to tell her to clean up.
I am tired of not having my own privacy.
I am tired of dealing with her attitude.

I am tired of waiting to go back to school,
It seems like the day is never going to come.
I feel like I am waiting for nothing doing virtual school...
I don't like missing the things I know
I won't be able to do my senior year.
I am tired of getting my hopes high.

I'm Tired Of
By C'myah Boyd (Grade 12)

I'm tired of being stereotyped.

I'm tired of being looked at
Because of my skin color.

I'm tired of being judged
Because of where I come from.

I'm tired of the stereotypes:
"GHETTO" "UNSUCCESSFUL" "POOR"

I'm tired of being treated unequally.

I'm tired of being counted out.

I would do anything to prove that those
Stereotypes are wrong.

I'm tired of being tired.

Money
By Kenyatta Cooper (Grade 12)

Money is hatred and death
People steal and kill for money
Money is evil
Money is life—something you can't live without
Money is chaotic and impure
Money is the world falling apart
Money is war and poverty
Money is cold and careless
Money is a lost love
Money is flames from houses burning up
Money is an unjust crime
Money is happiness from time to time
Money is a third world country
Money is a drought
Money is
Hell
The devil
A riot crowd
But money is something
You can't live without

I'm Tired Of
By Dominik Henderson (Grade 12)

I'm tired of shootings
In my community.
I'm tired of waking up
And finding out
Somebody I know
Is no longer here
Because of gun violence.

I'm tired of seeing mothers and fathers,
Etc…
Crying.
Nobody deserves to get their life
Taken from them.

I'm tired of HATE.
There's so much hate in my community
That's the cause of over half the
Killings…

Money
By Paul Hicks III (Grade 12)

Money can make you
belittle others, or
it can make you
fill others
with joy…

Money can destroy
someone's life, or
build
a great future.

Money can turn
a friend into
an enemy.

I Am Tired Of
By Ka'Veona Huddleston (Grade 12)

I'm tired of people.
I'm tired of everyone always on my case,
But not motivating me to do better.
I'm tired of everyone
Acting
Like they really care about me.
I'm tired of trying
To make people proud who don't recognize
The s*** I do.

I'm tired of school.
I'm tired of waking up early, like
I've been doing it for 12 years now.
I'm tired of falling off and trying to

Pick myself with non supportive teachers.
I'm tired of asking for forgiveness to catch up,
Because I feel depressed, and

I'm always hearing
"NO…"

I'm Tired Of
By Gregory Charles Jones (Grade 12)

I'm tired of looking down at myself.
I know that I'm much better.
Everyday is a competition with me.
Knowing that I can awaken.

I'm tired of conflict.
To me, they're meaningless bouts of anger.
Useless fighting, it solves nothing.
I'd prefer that everything's peaceful, so
There'd be no fear.
I'm tired of repeating.
Doing the same thing over and over.
I strive to be better and not be the same
As when I woke up this morning.
I love knowing there's things
I can do
That I can improve on.

I'm tired of being tired.
As much as I'd like things to be perfect,
I just have to wait.
Patience is key.
You can't live without it,
It's a virtue.
It's humanity's natural standard.

I Am From
By Kamerion Killman (Grade 9)

I am from swing sets flying in the air.
I am from reading books to
Seeing kids crying,
To playing with play dough.

I am from rules that teachers make,
To eating Sloppy Joes.
I am from lockers banking shut,
To smelling flowers.
I am from eating cereal to
Playing with board games.

I am from Homework and learning Life lessons.

I Am From
By Antonio Mendoza (Grade 9)

I Am From My Grandma's House,
Where I feel safe and protected. Where she told me to always be thankful, even for waking up. My grandma told me to stay away from trouble and never go down the wrong path.

I Am From Football,
I used to stay up late on Sunday nights watching football with my family. I grew up playing with friends in their yard playing for the Benton Harbor Tigers. When I play football, I get a joyful feeling inside my body, and it puts a smile on my face.

I Am From WWE Action Figures,
My friends and I would love to bring our favorite action figures to school and show them off. Sometimes we would trade and we would wait till lunchtime to play with them.

I Am From Fajitas,
Where my grandma and aunt used to cook beef and pork fajitas for cookouts. Fajitas are so good, I can eat them everyday and I won't get tired. Everytime they make fajitas, I always make sure I'm full. When I first tried fajitas, I realized that it was my favorite food and how

The good taste brought my family together.

I Am From
By Char'Naja Moody (Grade 9)

I am from my imagination,
All alone expressing my feelings
As I listen to music…
Khalani.

I am from crossword puzzles,
Trying to figure out every word, and
Left with no answers.

I am From the "wii" laughing and dancing,
And my face lit up like a Christmas tree.

I am from freeze tag,
Having all my friends come out to play,
Seeing big smiles as if our faces were about to explode!

I Am From
By Jo'Shaun Porter (Grade 9)

I am from Versace Cologne,
Bursting off of my magnetic shirt with a powerful smell...
Smelling so powerful, it can knock down trees.

I am from Shooting a Basketball,
Hearing the sound of the net when it goes in,
And pounding the ball on the long court.

I am from Seeing Butterflies,
Butterflies flying to beautiful, yellow and purple flowers.
I like seeing the flowers bloom.

I am from graduating from Eau Claire Elementary,

To going to middle school there, and
Doing hard work,
To move on to become a Benton Harbor Tiger.
All the while,
Eating burgers with tomatoes and jalapeños.
I am from life,
Where It's not easy...

I'm Tired Of
By Margaret (Big Margo) Pratt (Grade 12)

I'm tired of being tired.
I'm ready to succeed.
I'm tired of being angry and frustrated
For no reason.
I'm tired of being tired and
Feeling like I can't open up.

Parents half-way listen.
It's like it's through one ear and out the other.
I'm stronger than I look.
I always keep a secret place,
Because my conscious tries to hurt and
Say things like,
"You're not gonna make it. You're not good enough."

Well, I'm glad this place is secret.
That is where I know I can't give up.
I'm tired of being tired,
But that just another fight
I choose to confront my feelings, and
I will win every fight.

I Am From
By Avantae Ross (Grade 9)

I'm from watching WWE
I'm from watching WWE on Monday night with my cousin and my brother and asking my mom, "Can I stay up late and play wrestling with my cousin on the trampoline and have fun all night?"

I'm from Family Cookouts
I'm from enjoying laughter with family and friends over tender ribs, tasty chicken, and steaming hot dogs. After all the kids get done eating, we ride our bikes to the park. Sometimes we have to have family members sit on the handlebars to get there together. We are a team.

I'm from School Cookies
I'm from asking my dad for a dollar to buy some warm cookies from school, and thinking that I'm about to enjoy a soft and gooey cookie, then, as I am about to enjoy, I always hear someone ask, "Can I have a bite?"

I'm Tired
By Asia Tillman (Grade 12)

I'm tired of being misunderstood
And misread.
People think once I introduce myself
They know who I am off the bat.
Well, they are wrong…

I'm tired of being judged by adults
That are suppose to support me.
I'm tired of not having parents
Or anyone to depend on.
I'm tired of not having a shoulder to cry on,

But that's ok,
Because now

I cry alone proudly with my head held high…

I'm tired of school and its lack of education;
Teach me more…
I wanna learn the real things.

I'm tired of people pushing
Their religion
On me.

I'm tired of people judging me because I'm me,
And not anyone else.
I'm tired of not getting any sleep,
Because of all my worries that
I try not to worry about.

I'm tired of feeling like
Everyone else is fake, and
I'm only real.

I Am From…
By Tiania Tyson (Grade 9)

I am from…
Benton Harbor, where there are a lot of kids who don't know how their lives will be, because they were born here in Benton Harbor
And it's the only thing they know,
Where they don't know any better.

I am from...Hull International Academy,
Where they fight over the blue, plastic slides and the black swing set,
Where we play in the big field with our friends during recess.

Where kids fight like married couples.

I am from....A family where we all get together and eat and play freeze tag and dance to the Cha Cha Slide. Where we like to walk to the store and get hot fries and fruit.

I am from....A Christmas day, where my Auntie always makes her carmel cake and I eat watermelon, and where my uncles barbecue, while all the kids run around and yell and play, and where we open presents.

I am from where life is joyful when you have everything you need!!!!!!

I'm Tired Of
By Star Williams (Grade 12)

I am tired of wearing mask.
I am tired of having class,
Through a computer.

I am tired of being alone,
With no friends here to make
Me feel at home.

I am tired of feeling like a bump on the log,
While everyone around seem to be living

Their best life....
Ohhh...
I am so tired of this whole year.

Chapter Four
Looking Back, Looking Ahead

I Remember; I Don't Remember
By Teona Bell (Grade 12)

I remember having a day on the beach with my best friend. I remember how excited I
was when she told me she was coming to visit town. I remember how the hot sun was shining
the day she had arrived. I remember the 2 of us jumping into each other's arms, like little kids, when
we saw each other. I remember the drive to the beach, the windows were down, while the wind
bristled into the car.

I don't remember sweating at all that day. I don't remember any seagulls flying around us.
I don't remember having any melted ice cream. I don't remember meeting any rude
people on the beach. I don't remember regretting getting my hair wet. I do not remember the
time I had to say goodbye to my best friend the next day.

Untitled
By Jonairo Chatman (Grade 7)

I got a new bicycle last week
Just like my uncle promised
Cause I did something good
To finally ride to his house
To tell him thank you
And then go to my cousin's house
To show him my new bike
Then we'll go to the park
To meet friends and swing on the swings
Then we're gonna go to the bike park
And ride the ramps

(Inspiration, "Driver's License" by Olivia Rodrigo)

Jonario Chatman is an 11-year-old 7th grader at Fair Plain Middle School. He enjoys playing football.

I Remember; I Don't Remember
By Kenyatta Cooper (Grade 12)

I remember attending my grandpa's funeral. I felt distraught and sad. I remember we arrived late and sat in the back. I remember feeling confused when I saw him in his casket. He looked so different. I remember feeling hot when we were in Mississippi. I remember seeing my dad cry for the first time, because we were gonna come and see my grandpa before he died. I remember my sister crying because she couldn't see into the casket.

I don't remember what time we arrived at the funeral; I wasn't paying attention. I don't remember what we were wearing, because we were so young. I don't remember who else attended the funeral. I don't remember who gave his eulogy, because there were too many people speaking to remember. I don't remember how I felt leaving the funeral. I don't remember seeing his face anymore unless I see his face in a picture.

I Wish
By Monteonna Duckett (Grade 7)

I wish I had powers. If I was able to have one or two powers, it would be the ability to read the minds of humans/animals or the ability to fly. I want to be able to read minds with a twist though. I want to be able to control their minds too. Have you ever gotten into an argument with someone and wanted to know what they were thinking about you in their head? Well, I would KNOW!

Learning how to fly a plane would be cool, but being able to fly whenever I want, how high I want, and how low I want would be incredible! I would be able to fly over the world and oceans. I would be able to see everything I ever wanted to see.

Untitled
By Ar'Janiya Gray (Grade 7)

Some mean people be playing with people's feelings
And is just so, so sad
Because I'd be sad if somebody did that to me
I will be mad and sad.
So stop playing with people's feelings!

My Life
By Ar'Janiya Gray

My life is not always happy, but sometimes I am sad. Sometimes I am in my room in my book. So people are mean to me sometimes, but they don't know that they don't even really bother me anymore. My family makes me a little angry. So my life is not all good and not all bad. Sometimes it is just right. So that is my life.

Ar'Janiya Gray is a 12-year-old 7th grader at Fair Plain Middle School. She likes listening to music and dancing. She also enjoys reading, studying, and singing.

I Remember; I Don't Remember
By Paul Hicks III (Grade 12)

I Remember

I remember being left out of everything,
because I wasn't good enough or popular.
I remember being picked last for every team,
even when others were not as good as me.
I remember being the one who got picked on,
because I was an easy target.
I remember being the one who was always hated,
by people who were supposed to be my peers.

I don't remember my teammates trying to help me
get better…
or to try to help me pick my head up…
I don't remember them being happy for me when things
went good…
And I don't remember anyone being there to try to
Help Me
Get Better,
because they don't care…

I Remember; I Don't Remember
By Danny Jennings (Grade 12)

I remember about a month ago, I was giving my little sister a counseling session in the living room. I had no Idea where it was going at all. I just noticed through her behavior from the past couple of weeks, that:

1. She needed to get some things off of her chest.
2. She needed some great advice on how to react to the things that bother her.

As I attempted to give her advice, I remember she said, "Well, it's easier for you to have the mindset when you have 1,000 friends encouraging you to do better and be better!" At that moment, I just paused and stopped thinking of everything I wanted to say to her. After about 45 seconds of being still and speechless, I could only think of 1 out of those 1,000 friends that did the things that my younger sister said all of my friends do. I remember that even out of my oldest friends, I only had one who pushed me to be the best that I could be. I remember seeing that friend as a reward from GOD after giving my life to him.

I don't remember how we became friends whatsoever. I know we've known each other for over six years now. I don't remember really even talking to them when we first met. I don't even remember who talked to who first. We just suddenly clicked. After that, we just became the best of friends. I'm now here till this day and I still don't remember how I managed to have such a positive influence in my life.

I Wish
By Quentin Young-McCutchen (Grade 7)

I wish to be free!
Now, that can mean many different things
But I want to be free to voice my opinion Without any backlash or hate.
Don't you wish that too?
They tell you to say how you feel about some things
But your peers, friends, family
All think it's ugly
To you, it is beautiful.
That's what I wish
Complete freedom of speech.

Fitting In
By Antonio Mendoza (Grade 9)

There was one time, in fifth grade, I used to get bullied because of my skin color. I used to think to myself, "*Will I ever fit in...*" Sometimes, it would bring me down. They thought less of me, just because of the color of my skin. I didn't like that they judged me before they even knew me as a person.

I remember just walking down the hallway or gym and seeing people laugh and talk about me. The bullying would happen almost everyday, and I was getting tired. The teacher tried to help by moving me far away in class, but outside the class, the bullying would continue. Until this one day, I met a friend by the name of Julius Watkins, who stood up for me and introduced me to some of his friends.

He has always been a great friend to me since the day he stood up for me. Then I started to be happy and began to feel like I fit in. Julius told me, "Don't listen to those kinds of people, they just want to bring you down." He also told me, "If anyone says anything to you, I will be right there by your side."

I'm really thankful for Julius. He always knew how to make me smile and laugh. He made me feel like I never got bullied and made me more confident. I'm still friends with Julius Watkins till this day. I'm thankful he stepped up when no one else would and became a great friend to me.

White Lines in the Road
By Antonio Mendoza (Grade 9)

I looked both ways seeing if there were any cars passing by. I didn't see any cars, so I proceeded to skip on the path of the white lines and got to the other side of the road.

Open Door
By Char'Naja Moody (Grade 9)

Today I'm opening a door. A door to a better life. Having an open door is like not knowing what is going to happen to you. When the door closes, try knocking a few times, and if it doesn't open, let it stay closed.

A new door can't be opened until you're ready to close the one behind you forever. I am the open door.

I Remember; I Don't Remember
By Classie Newbern (Grade 12)

I remember being happy and waking up everyday with something to smile for and to lean back on my dad. You gave me that intake of happiness when I ain't know what being truly loved like a daughter was. You, my dear friend, was my best friend and a Step-Dad who treated me as if I was your own.

I remember going skating every weekend, then after, we would go to Family Video, and find us something funny to watch and eat popcorn with sugar covered strawberries and had good vibes flowing laughing all night long. I remember always scaring you with my funny pranks...sometimes they was a little extreme, but I didn't care at the time. My dear friend, I will always remember you and I hope from above, now that you are in Heaven, that you always remember me too.

I don't remember coming into this world with so many difficult challenges to face, waking every morning not knowing if it was going to be a good day or bad day. I don't remember having to go through so much hurting to realize your worth as a person. Me, wanting to have all the latest wardrobe or hairstyles to fit in and feel accepted by others, just so life could feel a little better. Even though having friends could be a good thing, I don't remember having somebody you called a friend. Then, the first argument you guys get in, they get turned on as if it was all planned.

In this generation we live in now, I barely remember good times when kids like us could just be kids, not having to worry about if they going to eat today, trying to find ways to help pay for family bills, or having to watch their siblings 'cause they mother will leave constantly like they was the oldest child. I don't remember more than I can remember, nowadays, life just ain't the same anymore without you. I don't know if I should be happy or cautious, just because I don't remember this "so called living life" ever feeling normal.

Boxed In
By Jo'Shawn Palmer (Grade 9)

Sometimes I do feel boxed in.
I feel boxed in when I don't get enough love,
When I don't have any money in my pocket, and
When somebody I care for dies.

I feel boxed in when I don't have a phone,
When I have to do school work, and when
I get hurt.
I feel boxed in when I miss something
Important, or
When I don't take a shower.

I feel boxed in when something of mine breaks.
I feel boxed in when I can't do what I want sometimes, and
When something I planned for don't go as planned, or when
I have to read.

I feel boxed in when my haircut is not crispy.
I feel boxed in when my shoes are not clean.
I feel boxed in when I have to clean things that smell bad,
When I misplace things, and
When I have to wear a mask, because
I can't breathe.

I feel boxed in when I don't color in the lines, or
When someone tells me I'm
Not old enough to do something.
I feel boxed in when I forget:
Phone chargers, phone, headphones, earrings, and cologne.

These are all of the things that make me feel

BOXED IN.

The Empty Street
Avontae Ross (Grade 9)

I looked both ways into the dark, empty street. The wind made a whistling sound throughout the neighborhood, and I crossed the mysterious street to go back home.

Photo credit: Gregory Charles Jones

Freedom Road
By Deshawn Swanson (Grade 9)

Durk was crossing the busy street and saw a Rottweiler foaming at the mouth and he got to running fast for freedom...

Crossing The Street Is A Mystery
By Kamerion Tillman (Grade 9)

Crossing the street is like a mystery of me not knowing half of the world and me crossing the street trying to go on a new adventure. Before I cross the street, I will be looking for new clues to get ahead of my adventure, not knowing what road I will take or if I would even make it to a new road. Yet, as I make my way across the street, not knowing my path isn't over yet.

Photo credit: Gregory Charles Jones

Crossing The Street For A New Life
By Tiania Tyson (Grade 9)

Crossing the street is like crossing the street for a new life. It is walking across the street without knowing what is happening next; no clue at all, and watching every step I take. I'm going across the street looking to see if anything is coming and looking both ways watching the traffic light. Me, zoning out of nowhere without knowing that I actually made it across to a new life.

Fitting In
By Tiania Tyson (Grade 9)

Do you ever feel like you don't belong?
Yes, I have felt like that, like I don't belong, like nobody wants me, and like there's some kind of animosity in the air.

It was my first day at a new school called Milwood Elementary. I was in 5th grade, and I didn't know nobody but my cousin, and we were in different grades, so I had to make new friends. Usually, it's not that hard for me to do, but at this school, it was hard. I was in two different classes with no idea of who to talk to or see. And for about a week, it was hard.

Everybody in my grade knew each other. They would be at lunch sitting together, talking together, and there I would be just sitting there with nothing to do but just eat. They would be at recess together, and I would be on the side-lines just looking/listening, until one day I came to school and the assignment was that we had to draw something and insert it on the computer as our home screen.

Somehow, when class was over, somebody walked up to me and her name was La'mya. She said she seen my picture and said that was the same thing she had thought of and did. She asked, "Do you want to sit with me and my friends at lunch?" I said, "Yeah." And for the next two weeks, I was with them at lunch, going to recess with them, and we got closer. We even end up finding out we stay right around the corner from each other. So we just hung out.

After that, we end up going to the same school for 6th grade, until I had to move down back to Benton Harbor for 7th grade. When I got back, I had to go to a new school, where I didn't know nobody but a few people, but I made new friends and it was easy this time, but the friends I was cool with in 5th and 6th grade, I still talk to them.
(cont'd)

The conclusion of this story is you just have to wait, get comfortable where you are, and it will get better.

I Wish
By Aubrey Watters (Grade 7)

I wish the killing would stop because there are too many kids dying at a young age—being taken from their parents. The killings are mostly just kids. I don't know why people think it is funny to go around killing people and taking them from their families.

There was this baby that went viral for trying to do the "young boy laugh" thing. Two days later he was killed in a drive-by shooting; his parents were very hurt. THIS is why killing people should not be an option.

I wish the killing and taking people from their family would stop. I don't think God made this world to be filled with killing people. Stop the violence and the world would be a better place.

Stuck in Life
By Javion Williams (Grade 9)

Sam prepared to go to sleep, turning out all the lights for early morning work, but it was so hot that she tossed and turned all night. So, when it was time to go to work, she got ready to go. She slugged out the door, but she forgot her car keys, because she was so tired. She was stuck...

I Remember; I Don't Remember
By Star Williams (Grade 12)

I remember the time I had a best friend...the time where I was so close to a person. I remember calling this person my sister because I had gained so much love and happiness from her! This person had my back and I had hers; we would go places together all the time and we even matched clothing a lot! I remember being there for this person whenever she was down and thinking negatively. I remember always motivating her and showing her how to love and feel confident about herself...

Oh, I remember them little arguments and making up literally 2 minutes later...I remember them 7 years fading away due to you getting closer to another girl. There was no more talking on the phone, no more asking to hang out, no more laughs, and no more real smiles...I remember everything feeling weird and different. I knew the friendship was coming to an end...

I don't remember you being there for me when I was down, even though I was always there for you whenever, no matter what it was. I don't remember the appreciation from everything I tried to teach you and make you happy with. I don't remember the last time you asked to spend quality time with just us as best friends. I don't remember the last time we actually had a real laugh. I don't remember the definition of "Sisters Forever"...I don't remember the feeling of having a bond with someone you truly loved and knew for many years, but I do remember losing the only friend I thought was real and the only friend who thought expressing my feelings was childish...that I remember...

Chapter Five
Nature Writings

Student authors clockwise from top: Antonio Mendoza and Jo'Shaun Palmer, Cha'Naja Moody, an empty chair, Javion Williams, Kamerion Tillman, Tiania Tyson, Avontae Ross

Lessons of the Seasons
By Teonna Bell (Grade 12)

Who made the bark on the trees?
Who made the crunching sound of old leaves?
Who made the whistling, rustling sound of wind?
The wind that blows the hardest during the winter.
The wind that makes us shiver.
The same wind who is making us rush to the store for comforting coats.
The wind that is covering our hands and ears with hats and gloves.
The wind is sometimes so strong, it uproots tall trees.
That cold wind soon starts to disappear...
That means a new season, my favorite part of the year.
I don't know why the colors of leaves change.
I don't know how the sky can go from gloomy to sunny.
I do know I enjoy switching my fashion according to the weather.
Tell me, should I think more deeply about the world & what it does?
Should I appreciate nature more, other than the clothes I buy for
A particular season?
Tell me, if I take the time to appreciate nature,
Will nature be as beautiful as I think it seems?

Teenage Mother
By Emaria Campbell (Grade 12)

Who made the baby?
Who made the baby upset?
Who made the mother cry?
This woman, I mean the one who sacrificed her young life,
She carried inside her this child for nine long months,
Who was kicking inside of her trying to come out.
Who is around now when this mother is down and needs lifting up.
I don't know exactly what a prayer is.
I do know how to be a mother to my child.
Tell me, I have a purpose now, because you were made for me.
Tell me to tattoo your name, so you will stay with me forever…

Country Life vs. City Life
By Emaria Campbell (Grade 12)

The shining sun in the clouds looms
Over the loud city…
The country is very quiet,
But the city is full of many riots.
Even though you may not know,
The country is the place to go to
Just get some peace…

But sometimes,
You might have to call and visit the beast,
Because the city is full of many exciting things…
You might even find your wedding ring,
But don't get caught up in the mix,
Or you might be doing six...

Both the city and the country
Have streets with bumps and curves,
And there's always someone you will find,
To get on your nerves…

Country vs. City
By Kenyatta Cooper (Grade 12)

City life is like the moon,
Vibrant, glowing, and proud.
It sleeps in the day and
Is awake all night.

Country life is like a hermit,
Only coming out when needed,
Quiet, calm, and peaceful.

City life is fun and flexing without rest.
Country life is horses and chickens and apple trees.

City and Country both go to the same school,
And both come with stress.
Both come with lessons and pain and regrets.
It's really all just the same...

Country Life vs. City Life
Janaha Ewing (Grade 12)

City life is where you hear crowds,
Country life is where you see clouds.
In the city you see cars.
In the country you see stars...

Mother Nature
By Paul Hicks III (Grade 12)

Who made humans?
Who made cats and dogs?
Who made Mother Nature?
Mother Nature, a woman of mystery,
The one who cares enough to keep you warm,
But can kill you with a freezing cold glare,
Who is trying to prepare you for the world,
But doesn't warn you of its dangers,
Who is bringing beautiful things to life just to kill them.
She lets her children make their own discoveries.
She lets them suffer from their own mistakes.
I don't know what true faith is.
I don't know how to be calm, to rest, to be assured of
My abilities, or how to believe that I'm good enough
To keep around, even though they don't want me to leave.
Tell me, what is the meaning of it all,
To live and learn or to wish you were never here?
Tell me, what do you believe is the purpose of life?

Metamorphosis
By Ka'Veona Huddleston (Grade 12)

Who made the moth?
Who made the caterpillar?
Who made the butterfly?
This butterfly, I mean
The one who grows from a walking insect into a butterfly.
The one who goes around drinking nectar from flowers,
Who eats on human's fabric and stinging humans,
Who is flying around with eye stunning colors,
As it flies to its next flower,
Soaring through the wind...
It arrives and drinks all the lovely nectar from the yellow mound.
I don't know how the flower holds its excessive amount of nectar.
I do know the butterfly flies as fast as a lion can roar,
Traveling the world in such short notice,
Being able to be free to the wind and sunny days,
Having family at every angle of the insect world.
Tell me, how is it to live so freely in the air?
Tell me, how is it to live with no pain?

Reckless Sunset
By Danny Jennings (Grade 12)

Who's responsible for making lying in the grass an activity?
Who decided to create an insect that sucks blood and leaves marks?
Who wanted me to have unbearable itches on the body?
Don't get me wrong, I love stargazing,
I love watching the sun rise and set,
But the extra complications irritate me.
Who is responsible for my irritation?
Who is the man in charge?
No disrespect, God, I just want to ask why.
Could you at least make the grass with a mixture of bug repellent?
I don't know why I'm even questioning you right now.
I don't know your reason behind it all.
You have never done anything that wasn't good.
With that being said, I do apologize.
Tell me though,
Tell me your plans.
I want to know your reason.
I hate being unaware of such things.

The Red Leaf
By Antonio Mendoza (Grade 9)

This leaf is the only red leaf I saw.
The leaf and I stand out,
Because we are different from others.

I spotted the leaf as it danced with the wind.
The red leaf is pointy, rough, and scratchy.
It sounds like sandpaper,
As I rubbed the leaf with my finger—connection.

The wind and leaf make me feel calm,
Because of how the leaf looks,
And how the wind brushes against my skin.

This red leaf taught me to be thankful for nature...
I am thankful for nature,
Because it is nice, calm, peaceful, and colorful.
It is my connection…

The Dandy, Dainty Dandelion
By Char'Naja Moody (Grade 9)

I am a soft, yellow flower
That blooms and soaks
In the Sun
With the love of other
Dandy, dainty dandelions.

When the wind blows,
I whistle,
Catching so much air
With a soft and gentle breeze…

I love how people are so drawn to me,
Because of my bright, glossy yellow.
It makes me feel so alive and joyful,
Until, I'm knocked back down to square
One
I am a dandy, dainty dandelion.

I go through many different stages and
Transformations...
That means my bright, yellow cuteness
Disappears,
And I change.
I just float away
In the air…

I guess I'm just the return and recycling of life...

Pollen.

Fall Is Approaching
By Classie Newbern (Grade 12)

Who made the season so cold?
Who made the great pumpkin patch and the scarecrows?
Who made the term *hibernation*?
I mean really why do animals have to gather up so much food to eat until
They are full,
Then after, sleep all the way to spring without waking up...
Seems impossible, right?
Who is going to protect them if they are endangered, but fast asleep?
Who is the name of the animals that are still
Up and moving around during hibernation?
Because they can't sleep until spring.
They have to eat to survive,
One meal ain't enough, so they hunt their prey down,
Even if it's cold or hot, they just try
To stick around.
I don't know how it feels to hibernate or if animals even like doing it or
Is it mandatory?
I do know fall is really beautiful when the leaves are falling on the ground,
And that's telling me the climate is changing.
Tell me, is there something else I'm missing about fall?
Tell me, what is your favorite thing about fall?
What about fall makes you want to question its season?

Brown Leaf
By Jo'Shaun Palmer (Grade 9)

The brown leaf look old and rusty,
But it feels laminated and moves in
Silence like ants.
I feel satisfied when I look at it.

My leaf sounds crunchy when I touch it.
It smells like burning wood and
Reminds me of the fall.

My leaf represents death, decay, and the coming of cold.
I connect with this leaf,
Because it's soft just like my hand.

I was drawn to this leaf because it has spikes on the side,
Making it different from the rest.

If I could get into the mind of this leaf,
I would think it looks at life like a balloon waiting to be popped.

I think this leaf feels sad inside,
Because it knows it's going to die out.

This leaf is like a pillow, how soft it is.
The tan, tinkle top of the leaf looks beautiful.

This leaf teaches me in life to never wait on things to come to you,
You have to go get it yourself.

Staghorn Sumac
By Avontae Ross (Grade 9)

Red like fine wine,
Peaceful like an ocean breeze,
Staghorn Sumac
Pops out a beautiful red color,
Contrasting against the green nature.

It gives out a natural smell.
It is protected,
Surrounded by the green leaves.

I feel calm near it, as I
Stare at the blue sky,
Seeing the bees go by,
Looking back to the
Furry red cone against the green,
Watching it
Moving with the wind,
Calmly whistling through the air...

The sights and sounds of nature draw me to them and are the most calming to me…

My Dead Leaf
By Kamerion Tillman (Grade 9)

The dead green leaf,
Lays on the ground,
Crumbled after being alive, and
Healthy in the tree.

Now it's rough, crunchy, and hard.
It has a musty, sweet smell.

It means fertility and growth.
It changes colors like mood swings.
It makes me happy.

I love playing with this dead leaf.
It looks at life all sad and alone.
It's a long lost leaf.

It teaches me a lesson in life to be happy with myself.

Photo supplied by author

Feather
By Tiania Tyson (Grade 9)

I am a Feather,
White and grey.
I am soft and light
When you touch me.
I fly when the wind hits me.

I am 8-16cm and
Really short, I know!!!
It's okay to be short.

I feel flimsy and sometimes I feel rough.
I whistle, rattle, and buzz.
Sometimes I smell junky, and
Sometimes I smell like flowers.

I symbolize strength, growth, hope and freedom.
I am a feather, who reminds people
Of acknowledgement,
And some people connect with me by spiritual realms,

Like a message from a loved one who has passed
Giving comfort…
Making people feel as if their loved ones are around…

I give

PEACE!!!

As a feather,
I draw people to me by
My attitude, values, beliefs and beauty.

I am a feather
Who teaches people that simple is better,
Or don't be afraid to borrow what works.

I am light as a new pen coming out the pack.
I am a healer...

Yellow Bloom
By Star Williams (Grade 12)

Who made the earth?
Who made the trees and the grass?
Who made the flower?
This vibrant yellow flower,
The one with the billowing blooms.
The one absorbing the yellow sunlight.
Who is the one flowing in the breeze;
Who is the one following the sun from rise to set?
Throughout the day, bees visit it to collect pollen.
I don't know how nature came to be.
I do know it is admirable, made up of a variety of unique things.
I enjoy nature...running through the grass and breathing in the fresh air,

Which I have been doing since I was a child.
Tell me, how else should I have spent my days,
Confined away in my room...
Tell me, how did you spend your premature life?

Chapter Six

Essays of Place
by 11th and 12th Grade Writers

Jealous
By Jakia Boatner

Sometimes I think my house is too colorful. I live in a tan and blue house with a big field across the street. My house has hardwood floors and carpet. My couch is blue with white and blue fur pillows. We have grey marble looking countertops. Our bathroom is blue, grey, and white. My dad's room is grey and white. He has some good grey dressers in his room. I like the way his dresser lights up. My room is pink, white, and black. I have three mirrors, but none of them cover my full body. The mirrors are white, pink, and black. One of my mom's room's walls is orange and the other ones are white. She has mirrors on the top of her bed. We have four rooms in our house and only one of them has a hardwood floor. I have a white and grey fan that my dad tries to take from me. We have a grey refrigerator and a white deep freezer. I have a 55-inch tv in my room and on my tv I'm playing music. My mom has a 65-inch tv in her room and she is watching *All American*. In our living room we have a 70-inch tv on our fireplace and Steve Wilkos is playing almost every morning. We have air freshener wall plugs everywhere around the house with cashmere fragrances. My house is a comfortable place for me, but I think I will be moving out next summer.

I feel like my house is a safe place for me because going outside in our city is really dangerous sometimes. We have a lot of shootings going on almost every day. I stay right next to somebody who is into some of the bad stuff going on right now, so coming outside is kind of scary at the moment. The crackheads here are just outrageous. They steal; they walk up on your porch to take mail; they ask and beg for money. That's why I stay in the house or go to Grand Rapids. I have family there, and when I need a break from Benton Harbor, that's where I go.

The only people that I allow to come to my house are my friends and my clients. My clients sometimes talk to me. Sometimes they are late to their appointments. My friends come over and sometimes they stay a night and we find things to make or cook. I make my friends cookies, etc. We talk about going to parties.

Another place I feel safe is The Body Gallery. When you first walk in you see walls full of pictures of tattoos that you can choose from, or you can have your own. There is a couch and a TV in the sitting room/living room. James is the owner and only artist. He has one wall in the living room with drawings. Then when you walk to the back, he has a bathroom and his work room. His work room has Marvel toys and posters. He has two black chairs in his work room. One of his black chairs is for piercings and the other chair is for tattoos. He plays rock music while he works. James has a big book where he writes all the appointments. It is on his table where his printer and cash register sit. James' tattoo room smells like chemicals or like green soap. Sometimes James is late to his shop or he leaves with a note on the door that makes people very mad. James also gives deals sometimes if he is late or missed your appointment. His shop is downtown by the dentist's place.

My first job was at Walmart; I actually liked working there when I first started. I was working in Lawn & Garden plus Apparel. I used to work every day during quarantine. I would only have like two or three days off. So after three months some people didn't really care about Corona. They would walk in Walmart without a mask and walk around coughing. There were just a lot of germs spreading around in Walmart. I would stay sanitized. There were hand sanitizer stations all over, and when I used to go on my break, I would clean the table that I was sitting at before I sat down to eat. Overall, it was a good place to work, even though there were some bad customers and circumstances. It was easy money. On holidays they would be very busy. One thing I loved is that on Christmas you would get a bonus on your check. One thing I hate though is when you're putting stuff back in order and people would take things they think they want to buy, then put it in the wrong spot or just throw it anywhere. I worked at Walmart for six months, and I had to quit because I was having a hard time finding a ride because my dad was getting sick and my mom had to work.

Another job I had was braiding for this hairstylist named Cassie Moore. I would wake up early in the morning; around nine she would pick me up and go to her shop downtown. She would pay me 15 or 20 dollars to braid her client's hair down how she wanted it. She still calls sometimes when she needs me to braid for her. Cassie has like six or seven clients a day. I actually love helping her because what she does helps me get better. She motivates me more and more. I watch and learn while she's doing the frontals and closures.

I have two friends in this town, their names are Quisha and Tyra. I've known Quisha since seventh grade, and I've known Tyra since eighth grade. Quisha and Tyra have the heart of a lion. We all became friends and became really close. My friends come over and sometimes they stay a night and we find things to do or cook. I make my friends chicken alfredo with Ro-Tel and bake them cookies, etc. We talk about going to parties. We also talk about moving in together and getting jobs. We live on different sides of town; I stay on the east side of town and they stay on the south side. We talk about our futures and what we want to be in the future. Quisha and I would like to be cosmetologists, and Tyra would like to be a masseuse. We also talk about moving into an apartment in Kalamazoo because there are apartments that are cheaper there and nicer. When we move I want us to rent a building for the talent that we have. I only want to stay there for two years and then move somewhere else that's bigger like Houston or Miami.

After I graduate I want to get a building where I can do hair and have people work for me that do hair and need a place to do hair. But before I try to move on to bigger things I want to be good at more hairstyles. I want to be good with melting a frontal or closure, learning to stitch braids, little braids. I kind of got the hang of the swoop ponytails, but I need more practice. I know how to do knotless braids, high ponytails, middle part ponytails, blunt cut ponytails, sew ins, feed ins and locs. For ponytails I use Got2b Spray and gel and edge control. For knotless braids and feed ins I use Shine n Jam and edge control. I get most of my products from the hair store or on Amazon, if I don't feel like going to the store. When I really start my business and I get everything settled, I want to do hair for four months of the year. You're probably wondering why I want to do this when I start. It's only because I have other things I would like to accomplish that I've been wanting to do since I was little, which is traveling to help the homeless. I hate to see people like that, so I would do a donation program for the people that barely eat or have clothes or have shoes. Then after four months I would do another round in the winter just so I won't be taking up a lot of time on just one thing. This is a long-term goal I have for my business. As long as everything goes well, I will be in a position to help other people.

My first time playing any sport was volleyball in eighth grade. It was a fun experience for it to be my first time playing. The only thing I didn't like was how the coach showed favoritism to other players. We had good games when we were out of town, but sometimes we would have bad games and be upset. I caught on when I first started, and I just practiced on days we didn't have practice, so I could be better. I also played volleyball in ninth grade, and it was just like eighth grade with the favoritism; the coach would only let certain teammates play. I just felt like everyone should've played because everyone has different skills and strengths. Later on in ninth grade I also did track. Now that was one of my favorites because everyone had to do something you could either do sprints, hurdles, distance, jumps, etc. I was doing the race. I wanted to do hurdles, but I said I was going to do it tenth grade year. But once Corona hit, that was risky.

Monday, July 26, 2021 I had done something I had never done before, which was throw a Nike red and white jacket out the high school window because the owner of the jacket kept hitting me and recording me and my friend on his phone. I let him slide the first time because I was doing my work. The second time he hit me again, and I tried to hit him back, but he ran in the hallway. So, the third time he hit me I grabbed his jacket and threw it out the window because he ran in the hallway again, so I couldn't hit him back. After he came back in the room, he grabbed my yellow hat off my head and ran in the hallway and went to the boys' bathroom. Tyra and I were trying to get it, but we couldn't because he was in the boys' bathroom. That's when we got in trouble and were about to get kicked out of school. They called our parents and told them what happened. So we ended up telling them that we were sorry for our actions and that we really needed summer school because online summer school doesn't motivate us.

My mom is the best mom I could ever ask for, not because she gives me money or buys me things, but because she's a strong person and loves her kids. She raised three kids and did a great job doing it. My mom is strong because on July 1, 2018 she lost her son, and my other brother was in prison at the time. I would have thought my mom would have lost it, just how I lost it, but she didn't. She was hurt badly but she kind of controlled it. She tried to help me with my problems even though we both were grieving. It took time for us to even go to therapy together because I used to cut my arms and do things to hurt myself and didn't want to talk to anybody because I was hurt so badly that all I could think about was releasing the pain on myself. His funeral day was tough. I was with my mom the whole time. Just walking into that place hurt me, and I know it hurt my mom too, but at that moment we had each other. This was our last time seeing him. We felt so empty and sad walking to see him in the casket; it just didn't feel real. My mom comforted me the whole day, and I comforted her until we went to the repast and home. A lot of family had come over and I couldn't take any more sadness, so I ended up going to my auntie's house to get fresh air.

I currently have thirteen tattoos, and only five of them really have a meaning to them. My first tattoo was two dice on my arm with my brother's name "Jojo" under it because before he passed away he used to love to gamble. My second tattoo is a heartbeat life line with my niece's name "Dream" in the middle. My third tattoo is a quote that says, "Learn from yesterday, live for today, hope for tomorrow" with lilies on my leg. That quote was meaningful to me because yesterday is the past, tomorrow's the future, but today is a gift. My fourth tattoo is my nephew's name "Jordan" and it's on the side of my face. My fifth tattoo is written in kanji letters and says, "love, beauty and happiness." That tattoo is on my back. The meaning of that tattoo is love is what I want after the things that happened to me. Beauty is something I fail to realize that I embodied because I had low self-esteem problems and needed to be reminded that I am beautiful inside and out. Happiness is what I want in life, since I just feel like my life is so sad. So basically that tattoo helps me motivate myself with being happy, feeling loved, and telling myself I'm beautiful.

When my auntie, my mom's sister, used to stay with us, she used to be in a hair class at Benton Harbor High School. I used to watch her when I was little and ask my mom if she would buy me a mannequin head just like hers so I can learn how to do hair. A couple days later she came home with one. When my auntie would have an assignment for that class dealing with the mannequin head, I would go get mine. I would watch her do one braid, and I'd do one braid. Then once I got the hang of it, I would just start practicing by myself, and I think I was like nine or ten years old when I was interested in doing hair. So the days she is not at home I will help myself learn different things about hair. I would also go on YouTube and watch videos about hair tips. I knew what I wanted to do early—doing hair just seemed so fun and creative. From me being so young learning how to braid and sew hair in, I'm actually proud that I had found something that I wanted to invest in. I watched and learned; it took time, but time was all I needed. Now I am better at braiding and doing other things. I have my own clients now, and I love making them happy when their hair is finished. It makes them want to come back to get their hair done again. I love my hustle. It inspires me.

My biggest pet peeves are when someone wakes me up out my sleep, eats my food, places my food touching other food on the plate, touches me with their feet, ignores what I have to say, talks over me when I'm talking, and being childish. Those things really annoy me and make me mad.

I had fun on my birthday. My birthday is June 23rd, and on the 18th of June, I celebrated my birthday in Grand Rapids. My cousin surprised me with a hotel room and gifts and food and drinks and a big cake. Quisha and Tyra came with me; we were all so pretty. Everyone was late, so when we got to my room, it was like 11pm. I started inviting people from Grand Rapids that I know. There were a lot of people there that made my night. So later, like around one something I fell off the bed and I broke my nail real badly. I was crying for so long because my real nail ended up coming up with my fake nail. There was a lot of blood. So then my cousin came with some band aids and wrapped my finger. She kept asking if I wanted to go to the hospital because I kept crying, but I told her no because I don't like hospitals, plus I didn't want them to because they were going to take my nail off, and I would rather let it to fall off. We went outside in the car. I needed some fresh air. We drove around for a little bit. So as I was crying in the car, my weird other cousin had something so smart to say that I didn't like. So we almost got to fighting. The whole time she was jealous of me; she was pulling weird stuff the whole time. So then I just told my cousin that did all of this hotel stuff for me to take me back to the room. I went back to the room, and everyone was gone when I got back. Tyra, Quisha, and my cousin Jamon were still there. They ended up giving me some pain pills, and I went to sleep for thirty minutes. When we woke up it was time to check out, so we cleaned the room and took all the decorations down. Then, my big cousin came to pick us up. She was mad because of what the jealous cousin said, and she went to where she was and talked bad to her—not just about what happened at the hotel room, but also about what happened between them, too. Then, we went back to her house downtown and we rode the scooters all around downtown Grand Rapids.

Untitled
By Denarion Evans

My home is light tan and pine green. When you first walk up to my house you see a little tree on the corner. My house has four bedrooms and one bathroom. All my walls are grey and the ceiling is white. I also have a basement and attic that are empty. When you first come in, you notice the living room. All decorations are dark hardwood brown and black and filled with pictures. The grass is nice and healthy green and stays cut, with flowers around the outside border of the front half of the house. When you're in my neighborhood you'll notice it's very nice in my area. Everyone's yard is cut and trimmed, filled with trees everywhere, with nice cool shade on the side of the roads. You also see a lot of construction signs because they are finishing the roads. All they're doing now is evening the dirt and putting grass seeding down.

Benton Harbor is broken down into four small groups: Eastside, Westside, Northside, and Southside. I'm on the Eastside. Some safe sides in the city of Benton Harbor are the West and Northside. Nothing really happens on the West or Northside, but there was one shooting, just one. On the other sides of town there are shootings monthly. Some danger zones are the Eastside at Highland and Buss, and the Southside at Broadway Park. The same things happen, multiple parties and shootings. Police are always called left and right for disturbances. There aren't really any exact spots that are dangerous; it's the sides that they split up in that creates the danger. So my advice is to be mindful and watch your surroundings because you could get robbed by anybody. Even the weakest looking person will surprise you when a gun is pulled. The situation in Benton Harbor can seem like too much. Since friend groups are fighting with each other, the problems can start in one place and end in another. Just don't feel too safe anywhere and put your pride aside. A person with a big heart in the wrong place is dangerous.

I only have four good neighbors—one behind my house and two across the street. The neighbor behind me is very cool, but I think he's a hoarder. Then the two across the street are both old, so they really don't come out like that. But both of them have unique yards filled with flowers and greenery. Both of their sons make sure their grass is cut every week. They are the only people that stop by my elder neighbors. The only time she really comes out is in the morning to get a fresh morning mist of air and to hear the beautiful birds chirping their morning songs. Then in the evening there are three little girls who live down the street and go bike riding. There are also neighbors on the Highland corner that are very cool. Their house is a mini mansion with a big yard all the way around. They just moved in last year, and that house belonged to the founders of Highland before they moved in.

I signed up for a maintenance job on the Indeed app. The app doesn't ask for any personal info, so you really could sign up for any job. My first job through the Indeed app was at Pilot Travel Center on 1860 E. Napier Ave. My trainer's name was Devon, a very caring person who wanted the best for the job. It was a pretty easy job for $10.27/hr. All I was doing was maintenance, fixing pumps, cleaning showers, and working both the box machine and garbage machine, etc. You had to be 18 to work there, and I was only 16. I worked there for a week and they gave me maintenance experience for the future. I will be looking forward to working there again when I turn 18. I also worked at another job I got from Indeed. I worked at the Berrien County Courthouse maintenance department dusting things, sweeping, mopping, and vacuuming all the offices. But of course I wasn't old enough, so the courthouse manager called me into the office laughing. He said, "You're not even old enough to be here." I had to leave on the spot. Then I called my ride to get picked up and collected my one week pay two days later. Working a job at the courthouse seems easy —everything is already clean and there is a lot of down time—easier than working at the truck stop. Both pilot and courthouse jobs have to do the same thing because they are both maintenance jobs.

New Fried Chicken (NFC) is at 610 E Napier Ave, Benton Harbor. It's right next to an arts and crafts school off of one of the busiest streets. It's not a normal restaurant. The menu is mixed with soul, fast, Asian, and middle-eastern food. The kitchen is busy, but it feels cool when you walk into the dining area to place your order. The place smells fresh with popping hot grease. The food doesn't take long. Even though it is a black owned business, there is a middle-aged man who tells customers, "10 minute wait." But no one minds waiting. NFC has a variety of everyone's favorite desserts and drinks -- caramel cake, carrot cake, chocolate cake, cherry cheesecake, and sweet potato pie, plus Pepsi products at the fountain. When you pull up it's usually packed because everybody loves the food. The only downfall is when you call in and order. The delivery time is around an hour and thirty minutes. But once you get your food, it's worth the wait.

Someone I know in town is my friend Doug, who is 18. He's like my brother. We grew up from fourth through eleventh grade. He is not very short, but he's also not very tall—about five eleven. His voice is very deep and with a little bit of rasp, which makes a perfect tone that makes his voice. He is very honest and down to the dirt, a loyal friend. He also has a hustler mindset, and he just wants to achieve success with his brothers. His swag, attitude, and mentality are unique and stand out. He gets it from his father; he also looks very similar to his father. I also have another friend DD and he is 17. He's quiet, nonchalant, and crazy. I also grew up with him in fourth grade too. He has anger issues to me, but to other people he's cool, but I know best though. He's not into hanging out with a lot of people. And looks like his mom a lot. He also has a lot of respect for elders.

My Aunt Shaneka is very open but can come off as mean to other people. Her personality is smart, curious, and funny. She's my grandma's second oldest child. She lives in an apartment complex. When my grandma died, Aunt Shaneka really was going through a lot. She was responsible for my grandma's things, all her belongings and bills. Dealing with all her siblings wanting something was stressing Aunt Shaneka out. She deals with a lot of depression, so she was taking a lot of trips. She went to Hawaii, the Bahamas, and California just to take her mind off things. She usually needs me to clean up because of her depression. She really doesn't feel like doing anything. I noticed the way she started to dress. She usually likes dressing up and going out of town a lot. But now she just puts on joggers and a t-shirt. I also noticed she didn't used to eat as much; now she eats a lot, constantly throughout the day. I really don't mind cleaning up. She pays me when I'm done, and she even gets both of us something to eat. Then she takes me home and makes sure I get there. She comes to get me every other Tuesday.

Where I have fun in Michigan is limited. I usually go to Grand Rapids, Mishawaka, or Kalamazoo because there's not really anything fun to do here but the movies and Hidden Point. You can race go-karts, play putt-putt golf, and hit baseballs in the batting cages. The problem is it's too small and no one really goes, so if you do it's vacant. So when I'm out of town, I go to Craigs Cruiser because they have everything: food, arcade games, ziplines, and outdoor/indoor go-karts. Also, they have good deals. I was supposed to go paintballing, but I never got the chance to go. I will before this year is over. I'm getting older, so I really did everything I wanted to do growing up. I've gone to the St. Joseph County Fair, movies, bowling, hotel parties, carnivals, etc. Most of the time I go to the mall or go shopping, look around, talk to new people, instead of having fun. Then you can't forget to get something to eat when you're out of town because their food is always better than Benton Harbor's fast foods. I woke up too late and missed school. It all started last night after the candle lighting. I felt everybody's feelings, I couldn't even cry. I never thought everybody would die. It started at 7, and I left at like 10:05. We just smoked and let the candles burn and his mom talked about him. Then I left and went home still thinking about my brother. So I smoked again with JJ and Molly Boy. And I just was up on a game until like 12, then I went to sleep without turning my alarm on. When I got up my OG said it's 8:30, so I got dressed and ready. Now it's 9:05; he is about to drop me off. We're at school it's 9:15 so Trooper Burton doesn't let me in. I really don't think 9:15 is a good time because it's just not enough time. But if the school closed its doors around 9:30 or 9:40, that would be perfect because it gives you the extra time you need to get ready because you're already running late. I just feel like 9:15 seems like it's too early and makes you rush if you don't ride the bus. And I usually walk there and ride home. I most definitely wouldn't have made it. I thanked my brother for trying to get me to school but my mom rushed him to put his stuff on and take me. But he wasn't ready so my mom stormed out the house mad because she wasn't ready either. On the way there she gave me a talk about how people don't like being rushed all the way there and back. So I instantly thought back. I woke up at 8:30 so there was no way I couldn't do everything. But I'll take the blame because my mom has a job to be at and I'm rushing everybody else because I didn't set my alarm last night.

When playing the game you are most likely online so you're going to need a mic. Because people don't like playing with people without a mic; it makes it harder to win without communication between teams. But the only way you can stay in a party without having a mic is if you're very good or you're somebody's friend and your friend tells the party host not to kick you out. Then the gaming community is just a whole different conversation because they will judge with ease. You have to learn how to just let s**t go and laugh or your gaming experience will be a hell hole. Then there are some games that are world famous and everybody plays -- Grand Theft Auto, Call of Duty, Apex Legends, 2k, Brawlhalla, etc. Then it also depends on what system you're on -- Pc, Xbox1/Xbox X, PS4/PS5. Everyone you know usually plays PS4. I have an Xbox because I grew up playing PlayStation. That's usually how the cycle goes for PS4 and 5 as well. But I don't really want to get into a debate because this debate could go on for forever on, which is a better system. PC is obviously not in the conversation because it clearly outperforms every statistic on both systems, and PCs are more expensive than a console. I'm going to switch to PC when I start streaming.

My goal in 2021 is to graduate on time for my mom. That's really the only reason I'm in school still. If it was up to me, I would've just let it go. Now, I'm just stacking my money until I feel like leaving my OG's krib. I am also working on becoming a man and putting my priorities first before anything. I am looking for a decent car for $5,000-$7,000. I want it to be the car I want and not a point-a-point-b car. Then after that I need to start looking for a house in Atlanta because I really don't want to live here. I want to move to Atlanta because the houses look way more modern. Also the neighborhoods are nicer, more calm, and more welcoming. It just looks better overall. The house and room sizes are also much bigger. I grew up in Benton Harbor from three months old until now, and I'm 17 now. I'll be damned if I'm stuck in Benton Harbor. All of my mom's kids moved out and went out of town and gave adulthood a try. I'm dropping my brand when I graduate, but I will be selling it through the school year. I really don't have an exact thing I want to do when I leave high school. I like to try new things. I accept leaving my comfort zone to make a living. But I got some ideas of things I want to do. I'm just already working on something now. When I leave, the last thing I want to see is my mom smiling because of the man I'm becoming and the man she made. So if she doesn't agree with me leaving I'm still leaving, and I hope I leave her with a smile. I'll be working very hard this year to make everything happen as planned.

There are a lot of things that I do in 24 hours to keep me busy. I usually listen to music, rap, or play games most of the time. I go outside every couple of hours to get some sunlight and fresh air. I usually just post up somewhere with my brothers. I never really like hanging with other people beside my kind or mess with the other side. I would rather go solo than mess with my brother's enemies. I never got the point of this. I like being around my brothers because it's not a safe feeling, it's more like everyone just sticking to the brotherhood. If I am not with them, I'm with my biological brothers. I usually just smoke and chill with them. Then if we go do something or plan to we make sure everything includes food and also a fun activity; then we just go roaming around. But he has friends so he is usually with them more than us. That taught me how to play my role and to not over play my role. My family and I do stuff together, but it's only like every other weekend, so we can have fun and plan it out fully. If not my mom will not get up. I really don't like having to plan with my mom because she will want to go one minute then she doesn't want to go the next minute later. So if she doesn't really want to go, I don't really get mad if she changes her mind because it's normal now. So I just let the day play out like it does because nothing was ever promised. So I just let things happen and hope for the best, but you have to be ready for the worst, too.

My wardrobe is different because my style is unique. It's very irregular because I like all the colors, especially bright, also custom colors. I usually get clothing depending on what others get. It's different but it works. So what everybody likes I don't get and the stuff they don't like I get. I'm the same way with shoes. I really don't want to go to Jordan's as my first choice. I'm a Nike type of guy, my favorite shoes are Nike SB Dunks. I admire the way they feel very comfortable there. Also I love the creativity and imagination they put into Nike SBS in general. Then the Off-White collab was the best thing they could've done—the design just fits the shoe so perfectly. They also give you a variety of colors of the Off-White zip tie. When I get my jeans I usually get pants. It doesn't matter the price or what brand because the pants are not that important when you're dressing up; it's the shirt and shoes that pop off the outfit, but they can't be regular or baggy jeans. I need to make sure they are fitted. Now when you get shirts you have to go classic with white and black t-shirts. Then, get a couple PacSun graphic t-shirts and some custom t-shirts you can make yourself or get them from the internet. With the custom t-shirts you can do almost anything you want because there's no right or wrong. Then the way I put outfits together it's different from others.

My summer hasn't been that fun, a lot has happened between 2019 and 2021. A countless number of family and friends have died, but I have adapted to it. It is sad the way everyone falls out because of differences, but it is what it is. All you can do is wait for everything to fall in place again.

Taking it to the Maxx
By Sean Sargeant

My mother just moved to a new house, and so far I like it. It's way quieter than my old house. I used to stay by Highland, and it was always loud. The only thing I don't like about the new house is that it's always hot in my room. When I'm home, I always leave my fan in the window because my room is always hot like two fat people in a sauna. My new room is so big—I have white walls and a big bed with a black tv stand. My sister and I finally got our own bathroom, and it has a big mirror, a marble countertop, and a nice shower.

I really don't know a lot of people who stay out there. I only know Devin, D'erica, and Kevin. When I decide to go outside, I'll either go to Devin's house to kill him in 2K or I'll go to Kevin's house and hoop. I have never been to D'erica's house before, but I know somebody that did. It is only the little kids that stay out there, that's why I really don't go outside. I would go outside everyday if there were kids my age out there.

Usually I'll get a ride around town by my mom, dad, step-dad, step-mom, grandma, or my friends ,but if it ain't far I'll just walk. Sometimes I'll just walk to waste time.

Honestly, Benton Harbor isn't all that dangerous. It's just people being at the wrong place at the wrong time. Many people gather in the wrong places late at night. There really isn't anywhere dangerous if you stay out of street beef. Highland, Benton Manor, and Union Park are somewhat dangerous because people gather and party. These places aren't really dangerous; they are just places where something is more likely to happen. To me, everywhere in Benton Harbor feels like a safe place, if you stay out of street beef. Some of the safest places to me are the high school, Teen Center, football field, and the baseball field. There's more than that, but if I'm not at one of them, I'm at home or my girl E'moine's house.

Another safe place would be my girlfriend's house. I feel like our relationship is good because we really never argue and we damn near act like best friends. When I am over her house we'll try to find something to watch, but we can never agree. I want to watch anime, but she wants to watch *Twilight*, and that show is so weak. We'll end up taking turns putting on a show we want to watch. But at the end of the day, she always makes me happy, and that's what I care about. She's my little ride-or-die for real!

I work at T.J.Maxx. It's always cold to me. People say we have the best customer service and we are a good store. When I clock in, I always keep the store clean, and I sometimes try to make work fun because it's always boring there. I like working at the Maxx with Mike. He always has me crying laughing when we work together. The other people I work with are cool as hell too. They are always laughing and acting funny too.

When I clock in at the Maxx I'm either working with my girlfriend E'moine or my homeboy Mike. No matter who I work with, they both make me laugh. When I'm with E'moine we are always fighting or hitting each other with stuff in the store. Then when I work with Mike we be doing stupid stuff. Like one time he was chasing me around the store saying take a picture, and we were crying laughing. There's another person I work with. I call her M bandz. That's Mike's favorite friend; she's the funniest girl in the Maxx.

My first job before T.J.Maxx was a janitor. It was easy. I used to clean up places like the Teen Center and the Little Club. I used to work with Lexi, and we were always laughing because everything was funny to her. When we weren't working with each other, I would just listen to my favorite song called High Speed by G Herbo, and I'd be lit at work the whole time.

It feels like I am always at Mike's house, that's really my second house. When I'm over there he and I always try to find something to do. I was at his house this whole weekend, and all we did was have fun. Thursday, we had a 7v7 football game at Lakeshore, then after that we went to Burger King for some food, then we went back to Mike's house to play Call of Duty Warzone and chill. Friday we didn't really do anything but go to work and play the game. Saturday, we went to work in the morning and after work we went to our friend Justin's house, and we were chilling over there. Justin told some girls to come over. Then when the girls got over there I left and went to my girlfriend's house. Sunday, I chilled with my girl for a minute, then I went back to Mike's house, and we played the game all day.

To me I feel like I'm the most hard-working basketball, football, and baseball player in high school. My work ethic is crazy. I really don't get tired of working hard because I know somebody else out there is working harder than me. I use sports to escape reality because without sports life would be really boring.

For these 3 years of high school I've enjoyed playing basketball with my friends and coaches. Freshman and sophomore years, Coach Mike showed me that hard work will get you somewhere. After we lost our first game freshman year, the next day at practice Coach Mike made us run the whole practice so we could get in shape. Then, right after running we went to the weight room and Coach Mike made us do 100 pull-ups. Then, after that we never lost another game. Junior year, Coach Nelson showed me how to be disciplined. Coach Nelson really got on us because of the little things—he would tell us to get behind the line. If we were on the line, we would run. Then, if he told us to run and we jogged, we would have to do a down and back. Then this summer, Coach Sterling showed me togetherness and brotherhood. During the summer we went to Detroit, and we all were in a hotel. We really got to know each other with all of the talking. Then after we got done talking, we went to the Detroit Tigers game.

I've enjoyed playing football too, but football is when you see a different OJ Sparks (me). Friend night is over when those game lights come on. I'm someone different on the field. You'll think you never knew me before. All my coaches from football show me lessons too, but it's really the same thing for basketball. Coaches really said, "Don't nobody else got your back but the team."

This football season is going to be crazy. Our opening game is against Berrien Springs; then after that, we play Ottawa Hills. This is going to be a good game because they are just like our high school. Then after that, we play South Haven at home. That game is going to be crazy too because they were talking stuff at the 7v7 practice games this summer. This year's drip is going to be different, just stay tuned and watch this movie.

Something that really helps me throw out my everyday life is music. No matter how I'm feeling, music can always change my mood. I really listen to music every day. I probably listen to over 300 songs a day. My top five favorite songs right now are Bloody Canvas by Polo G, 5500 Degrees by EST Gee, Pride Is the Devil by J Cole, Had To by Tee Grizzley, and Danger by NBA Youngboy. I don't only listen to rap either, I listen to all types of music.

After high school I want to go to college. My dream college is Ohio State. It would be nice If I get an offer from them, but if not, I'll still go as a walk-on. I'm really ready to go to college anywhere. If the college has what I'm looking for, I'm ready. I'm going to college for accounting or sports management. I'll study accounting because I'm good with numbers. My favorite subject has always been math. My eighth grade class at ACA went to LMC and there was a teacher there who gave us a math problem. I got it right, and I kept answering all the questions that he asked. Then he said, "You should go to college for accounting." I did every sport in high school but wrestling. I figure I might as well do sports management. Coach Sterling really was the person who gave me the idea for sports management. He said, "Since you do all them sports you should know a lot about sports history and you're a good student. You should look in at sports management for college."

After college if I'm not playing in the NBA or NFL, I'll become a carpenter, accountant, coach, or a business owner. I'll become a carpenter because I kind of know what to do. I used to work with my uncle on houses. We put up drywall, put in new flooring, did the plumbing work, and did the electrical work. Like the professor who gave me the idea of becoming an accountant, my uncle gave me the idea of becoming a carpenter. I would like to become a coach, so I can show kids how to make it to the next level. I always wanted to be my own boss. I just want the freedom to not have to listen to anybody and the freedom to stop and start my work whenever I want. Being my own boss would have its advantages.

Recently at the Maxx, Mike got fired for arguing with a manager and she really is not even a manager. She is a key carrier, but that day all the managers were off, so she was the next person up. I wasn't there when it happened, but I know how she is, and I know how Mike is. I really think she is picking on people and when she is the manager she is running the whole store wrong. We got areas in the store. Like I'm usually in Home. then there's somebody in Women's, Men's, Kids',

Jewelry, Beauty, and the front of the store. She would put everybody in one place basically that's busy, and that's so wrong.

My favorite superhero is Captain America. He first appeared in March 1941 in the comics. His first movie appearance was July 19, 2011. This story is about a kid named Steve Rogers who joins the army and volunteers for an experimental super-soldier serum. After he took the serum he got real strong then after that was saving people. After World War II he was flying somewhere—I forget—but he ended up freezing for like 15 years.

When I get bored and I'm at home I'll play the game, go outside, or facetime E'moine to see what she is doing. My favorite game is Skate 3. It's about being a skateboarder. You go skateboarding to try to get money for your skate company. When I get bored at school I'll listen to music and just walk around or try to go to the gym and shoot around. I'll only do that when I get done with all my work.
My favorite shoe brand is Jordan. I just like the way they make their shoes. I've been wearing Jordans since I was little. I think my first pair of shoes was some Jordans. My top five favorite shoes are 13s, 11s, 4s, 1s, or 12s. I had every pair of shoes but some 2s, 3s, and 14s, but all the shoes from 1-14 are the best shoes to wear. My favorite shoe of all time is the black Levi's denim 4s, the colorway is so hard, and this is a collaboration with Levi's.

I haven't watched regular cable tv in so long. I really like streaming platforms like Netflix, Hulu, HBO Max, and Amazon Prime. All I really watch is anime or some good movies. The anime I watch are Dragon Ball Z, Attack on Titans, My Hero Academia and sometimes the teenage mutant ninja turtles but that really ain't a anime. Last night I watched Gemini Man. It was a good movie. It's about a really good soldier that was gettin' old so they were trying to make a lot of robot versions of him, but they were bad so he killed them.

My dream college is Ohio State University. My momma is the real reason why I like them is because growing up that was the only college we watched. I think I look good in scarlet and gray, but besides sports Ohio State University is a really good school. Fun fact: Ohio State University was founded in 1804 at Athens and is recognized as the first university in Ohio and in the Northwest Territory. If they don't accept me in Ohio State University, I'll go to a HBCU and the school I'll go to is South Carolina A&T University.

They Were Not Ready
By Tyra Williams

I live near a big field filled with flowers and grass. My house has two stories, and all the rooms have brown wooden floors. Our living room is the first room in the house. The walls are painted white, and all the furniture and decorations are grey or black, which are my mom's favorite colors. Our kitchen is the same with white walls and black cabinets and countertops. Our bathroom is painted blue with pictures of flowers. My room is painted pink, because pink is my favorite color. My sister's room matches the bathroom—it's blue with flowers. My other sister's room is pink and blue. My mom's room matches the living room because those are her favorite colors. The downstairs has air conditioning, which is why I stay downstairs most of the summer. My backyard is as big as the field next door with a storage house we keep stuff in. My mom, my sisters, and I love living there.

We feel safe there because it's a place where we've been at our lowest and at our highest. Being at our lowest helped us a lot because being at your lowest teaches you how to get to your highest. And when we came to our highest it showed that we could handle anything. It helps when I feel like I'm failing. It gives me motivation, plus I feel loved and protected by my mom and siblings. But, where I don't feel safe is the streets near me because of a lot of gun violence and other things like crack heads that stand outside of the stores, which are also near me. And another thing that makes me feel unsafe is the deaths that keep happening every other week. I really hope my family and I move one day.

When we move I'm going to miss some of my neighbors, especially the dude that looks like he is in his 30s and comes down to my house every other week with a big red truck to do our yard. Sometimes I think he has a crush on my mom because he does the work for free, which is something you don't see every day. I'm going to also miss the kids across the street who come to play with my little sister in the field next to my house. They are running around yelling and playing tag or they are on their bikes half of the time. The field next to my house is another thing I'm going to miss. It always helps us out with events such as open houses or parties. I'm going to miss the way our street is because it's really big and wide with no potholes, which makes it fun to fly down the street really fast. Flying down the street isn't a good thing, but when you live in Benton Harbor it is, because there's nothing else to do. That's the closest you can get to a rollercoaster, but the thing is you can't do that on other streets because in our city the roads are really bad, which is why I love my street.

The weirdest place I've ever been in Benton Harbor is The Body Gallery, a tattoo shop down near the police station downtown. I wouldn't say it's a weird place, but it's a place with a weird feeling. It's a comfortable place to be, which is the good thing, but as soon as the needles sink in it feels weird. James is the owner and the only worker there, so he is very busy, and it's hard to book an appointment with him. He has done all my tattoos. My favorite tattoo is the rose with my grandma's name on my right arm. He did a very good job and gave it detail. James makes you feel at home.

Another weird place is the creepy gas station downtown that most people don't know about. It has paint falling off the roof and bugs flying everywhere. I even saw a mouse run across the doorway really fast from a bag of cheese chips someone left open on the ground—nasty, right? And when the worker talks, he slobbers everywhere. The crazy part is I saw all that in one day because after that I never showed my face there again.

My first job was a summer job where Jakia and I went to the parks with lunches for the kids and games for them to play. We were separated by groups of ten kids. Jakia was placed at Broadway Park, and I was placed at Union Park. The saddest part is I was separated from my friends. So I had to introduce myself to new people to meet new friends. I met a girl my age named Asia. She was very good with kids, which is something we both loved. Every Tuesday this little girl came to me and Asia. Then one day she introduced herself, but she seemed scared to talk to other people except for us, so we had made our own sitting area, brought some food and toys to her, then just sat there to make her feel comfortable. The little girl was a very kind person. She thought so much of other people and could laugh for hours. But as soon as someone else came around she was back to being quiet and shy. So I pulled her to the side and asked if she was okay. She said, "Yes, I'm shy." I thought I would just give her a couple days to talk to other kids. But one Tuesday she stopped coming. I was confused about where she was until one day this little boy named Chris walked up to me, and said, "Hey, are you Tyra?" I said, "Yes." He said, "Asia wanted me to tell you that the little girl moved to Grand Rapids." I asked him if they were related, and he said, "Yes, that's my sister, but she's moving with my dad." So then I asked if he could take her some homemade food and toys. He agreed, and I could understand that people wanted to move away from Benton Harbor, so I was happy that her family made that decision.

I only have two friends, but they are the coolest friends you could ask for. I met Jakia in 8th grade, and I met Quisha in the 9th, which isn't really that long ago, but we have way more years to go. They are really fun and playful. They joke all day over little things. For instance, if they saw a cat running down the street they would have something funny to say like "that cat runs like Mose." Jakia and Quisha are like a friend in one; they give out the same vibes. My family enjoys having them around, which is surprising because my family really didn't like the friends I had in the past. I never understood why. Now that I have gotten older, I see a lot more and realize a lot, which took me a long time to understand, but my friends I have right now are as spoiled as they get. I love having them around. Even when I'm feeling down, they find a way to make me laugh and bring happiness around me. I never had to question their loyalty and they never had to question mine. Don't get me wrong, they do get on my nerves, but they wouldn't be real friends if they didn't, because real friends have disagreements; well, that's what I grew up to know.

It's always something different each school year, but school is still my place. Freshman year was full of surprises and excitement, but it was also scary because it was all new, and I was growing up, so I had more responsibility and I found out who my real friends were and who were not my real friends. When sophomore year came I knew what to expect and I knew how to handle things more responsibly, which made sophomore year one of the best school years. I started playing sports, which is something I thought I'd never do, but turns out it was fun. I learned that it was better to hang alone at school which was easy because I have siblings to go home to. Junior year was one of the worst! We couldn't come into the school building which made me fail classes because I'm not really good with computer work. I started coming to summer school which helped a lot. Now I'm on track for senior year, and I have a good feeling senior year is about to be a lot like freshman year with even more surprises, but I'm going to make smarter choices by focusing on just school work. That was hard for me to do at first, but I realized that all the other stuff like friends, boys, getting suspended, all didn't matter anymore because eventually I'm going to graduate and never have to attend school again, so it's better that I finish out strong and show people I can do it!

I dislike animals. First, let's talk about lions. I learned a lot about them in school. I just think they're bullies and that they try to be bullies on purpose because they know they can from how big and scary they look. Lions have a muscular, deep-chested body, short, rounded head, round ears and an enormous mouth with fangs as big as fingers. Doesn't sound too pretty, right? I also dislike dogs and cats. I wouldn't say I dislike all dogs. The small, fluffy, cute dogs are okay, but the majority of dogs, like big dogs for some reason, you always have to beware of them because they always seem to be mad. Plus, too many people tell me stories about getting attacked by them, and I never would like to feel that type of pain. Cats are just weird. They sit around staring. I used to have a cat years ago. He liked to ambush me. When I woke up for school the cat would jump on me, when I came home from school the cat would jump on me, or on the way to the bathroom the cat would jump on me. My mom said it's because he was scared and didn't know it was me, but it still didn't matter to me because I'm just not a cat person. I could never see myself with a cat again. Last but not least, I hate insects. I don't know if insects are considered animals, but I hate insects anyways because they are always in the way and they give me a creepy feeling. Have you ever been minding your business then suddenly a fly or bee comes flying around your head or have you opened your front door at home and a fly comes in, then out of nowhere there are like ten flies, or maybe I'm exaggerating just a little? Those are the most annoying things that could happen to a person who does not like insects at all.

Some of the places in town that I love to eat at are Pizza Hut, Burger King, Sharks and Applebee's. Pizza Hut is an American multinational restaurant chain and international franchise founded in 1958. I know that because my cousin works there, and she loves her job a lot and wants me to work there too, but I just want the food. I really enjoy their pizza and hot wings after a hard day or anytime I'm really hungry and want a lot of food. Not too many people can eat a pizza by themselves. And no, I didn't eat it all at once. I saved some for later. Burger King is cool. I love their burgers, but I don't really want to talk about Burger King right now because at the moment I'm really mad at them because the ice cream machine is always down, and it is way too hot for that to be happening. I love Sharks a lot. I can honestly say Sharks is my favorite! If you don't know Sharks, it's a place that sells chicken and fries which is crazy because I really don't like chicken, but it's something about sharks that makes me come back. Sometimes my friends and I would go get some Sharks after school and just park outside of Sharks and eat which is fat, but we were just bored. I saved Applebee's for last because there's only one thing I'll eat there, and that's the alfredo. Sometimes I'll eat the boneless hot wings but that's pretty much it. It's not because they're nasty. I just never tried eating anything else from there, but I'm going there this weekend, so I'll try out their burgers or chicken tenders or maybe even the roast with shrimp. I'm really not sure yet because Applebee's has so many options.

Benton Harbor creeps make me want to move, but creeps aren't a nice thing to say, so I'll just say people that don't have their life together and aren't ready for the real world and who are around the age of 30 to 50. They stand outside of stores which is weird. They always ask me for money, and as the good person that I am, I'll always give it to them. I always wanted to grow up helping people like that, but one day I didn't have money on me, and a man outside of BJ's got upset. If you don't know what BJ's is, it's a store on Empire near the high school. I never understood why he got upset, but as I sat and thought to myself, I started to understand more and I feel like the reason for him getting mad was because he was stressed. From the looks of his clothes vs. others' he was the most decent one. I had seen him walk to a car, and I feel like his attitude is the way it is because of the way he had grown up. When I came back the next day, the man wasn't anywhere to be found, even after weeks of coming. So, as I was walking in the store I overheard a women say, "I'm happy all the weird creeps are gone," and the person next to her laughed trying to cover up her mouth and said, "What happen to them, girl?" She shrugged her shoulders and said, "I think they got their life together finally." I don't know if that's true, but something in me believes that it is from the clothes he had on, and hopefully it is.

The dumbest thing I ever did was go to a party. Don't get me wrong I go to parties all time, but this one was different because I had this feeling in my gut that I shouldn't go. I did anyway because I didn't want to be a party pooper. When we first got there I stayed in the car. I was on my phone texting my sister about a big trip we have coming up. Something told me to check the time. It was 10:20 PM, so five minutes later at 10:25 PM my friends came to the car telling me to get out and join the party. So I listened and got out to have fun. I'm at the party dancing around with my friends rapping to Rio da Young OG. If you don't know who that is, he's a 26-year-old American rapper, best known for his album "City on My Back." He was born in Flint on May 11, 1994. I listen to his songs a lot. Well, okay enough about him. So as we rapped for hours and hours people started to leave. Eventually we caught the memo and decided to leave also. We walked to the car, but the doors were locked. I started looking for the keys. I checked my purse, and still no signs of the keys. I sat and thought, "If I didn't get the keys and I was the last one in the car, where would they be?" Something told me to look through the glass window and there they were on the driver's seat where I was sitting.

Pretty smart right? I paused and instantly started to freak out because the car was my sister's and she already wasn't sure about me driving because she was out of town, then this happened! Like are you serious? I checked the time. It was 5:00 in the morning and my sister would be home at 8:00, so I had to figure out what I was going to do in three hours. A couple of minutes later two men were walking. I stopped them and asked for help. Luckily they were nice people and decided to help. As they helped me I saw that the car was starting to look funny. As I started to move closer I started to smell liquor. I whispered to my friend telling her that I think they are drunk, and she had the same feeling also. I walked up even closer and saw that they were messing up the car. A piece of the car was falling off and the door was bent. After that I completely lost it. I started to cry, and I started to cry harder as I looked at the time; it was 6:40. I told the two men to stop because they didn't know what they were doing. They were drunk so they instantly stopped. One of them even said, "man I'm so drunk." LIKE WHAT? I didn't let it get to me because I still had hope that everything was going to be okay. It was a good thing they left though I honestly think the only reason they stopped and left as fast as they did is because they saw that we were girls, and we all know what that means. So I sat there calling the police to help me.

Instead a man came walking up with tools who looked like he was the only one with common sense around at the time. He asked if he could help. I instantly thought he was drunk too for a minute, but turns out I was wrong. 30 minutes went by and he opened the door so fast without messing anything else up. My friends and I jumped up and down saying thank you to the top of our lungs. I believe one of my friends even hugged him. When I got in the car I realized that the car was all messed up from the two men earlier. I instantly got sad again and I thought there was nothing else I could do in time. I'm sitting in the car trying to figure out what can be done. I got a text from an older guy friend that sells cars. I didn't get my hopes up yet because I wasn't sure if he knew how to fix cars. I just thought he was selling them. This is why you shouldn't judge a book by its cover. I finally asked if he could take a look at the car for me. He replied yes then sent his location. I immediately drove to him as fast as possible.

When I arrived the first thing he said was, "Dang Tyra, you look like you haven't had any type of sleep, did you go to the party last night?" I paused and thought to myself like wow, I really haven't had any sleep, which made me mad because I regret going to the party so much. He looked at the door and said he could fix it, which he did! I was so excited that I could hug him, which is surprising because I really don't like hugging people, but at that moment I didn't care. I gave him the biggest hug ever and thanked him 100 times. I got in the car and started to drive home. As I'm pulling in the driveway to my house, I noticed a car with tinted windows, so it was hard for me to see inside. I was so busy that I lost track of time. I looked at my phone. It was 8:10 AM and as soon as I looked up at the car, I saw my sister. I got out of the car and we met at the door at the same time. I had a nervous look on my face. She asked where I had just come from and why I was looking that nervous. I couldn't tell her, so I started from the beginning and told her everything. She was mad at first, but she eventually got over it. Then everything went back to normal, but one thing I'll never do again is go to a party. That ruined it all for me.

Chapter Seven
Believing, Hoping, and Dreaming

I Believe
By Teona Bell (Grade 12)

I believe in Aliens.
I believe in Aliens because
I do not believe we are the only species out there.
I believe in Aliens because only 4% of space has been explored.
I believe in Aliens because there is so much
More of the world to be discovered.

I believe in fate.
I believe in fate, because
I think everything happens for a reason.
I believe if you are supposed to have something,
You will have it.
I believe that if it is meant for you, it will happen,
In minutes or even years.

I believe in love.
I believe this is something all humans experience.

I believe this is something everyone craves.
I believe it is more of a thought at first, then a feeling.

I believe in God.
I believe in God, because I feel his presence.
I believe in God, because I took the time to learn for myself.
I believe in God, because this is a big world & you don't know
What could exist & what could not.

I Hope For
By C'myah Boyd (Grade 12)

I hope for happiness.

I hope that this story has a
Happy Ending.

In life,
People go through things:
Family problems, heart breaks, struggles…

I hope for everything to be
Worth it
In the end.

I hope for all of my dreams
To come true.
I hope all of the hard work pays off.
I hope for success.

I hope for all of my problems and struggles
To become happiness.

I Believe
By C'myah Boyd (Grade 12)

I believe in success.

I believe that everyone can be successful,
No matter what they have been through
Or where they're from.

I believe that success comes with
Time and Patience.

I believe that anyone can be successful
And strive for greatness
If they just put their minds to it.

I believe success is easy.

I Believe
By Emaria Campbell (Grade 12)

I believe there are Mermaids,
Their voices are beautiful.

I believe in ghosts,
They use your mind as their hosts,
They scare people sometimes.

I believe there are angels.
They help you out from many angles,
Even when you think you're alone,
They will always be there to carry you home.

I believe we should fight for our rights,
We will be alright,
You might not see light,
But keep going like a knight...

I Believe
By Christine Gonzalez-Stubbs (Grade 12)

I believe that if you are respectful,
You get nice things,
Like a nice car,
Houses,
And other stuff.

I believe that if you are not being respectful,
You don't get nice things in
Life.

I Believe
By Dominik Henderson (Grade 12)

I believe in myself.
I believe that
I can do anything
I put my mind to.

I believe I can work
Hard on a consistent basis.
I believe in my work ethic
For football—
I can be really great.

Even if football doesn't
Work out,
I still believe I can be
Successful.

I Hope For
By Gregory Charles Jones (Grade 12)

I hope for drastic change.
So much anger in the world
Negativity, death, and destruction.
In the media, that's all we hear.

I hope for world peace.
That'd be a hard battle to fight.
But we have to start somewhere.
War is not the answer.

I hope for salvation.
On this little planet called Earth.
Conflict isn't what my Father intended.
Humanity should learn their worth.

I hope for respect and kindness.
It's not hard to do.
We just have to believe in ourselves.
Each and every one of us is special.

I Believe
By Gregory Charles Jones (Grade 12)

I believe in change, and
True thoughts about becoming better.
Believing deep within yourself in what
You thought was impossible.
Transforming into something new, something
You thought you could never…

I believe in recreation;
Becoming an all-new person.
Turning the bad into good.
Turning the old into new.
Changing to something, day-by-day, while
The sky's still blue.

I believe in dark and light.
Some days you feel down and some days
You feel up.
What matters in the end is that you keep
Going.

Achieve your goals, make new ones, aim to be
Better, then become better…

I believe in right and wrong.
We all know nobody's perfect.
It takes many failures before becoming
Successful.

What matters is that you correct it.

Dream House
By Antonio Mendoza (Grade 9)

I want a big, white house with a door as huge as an elephant. I also want a huge yard with nice red roses. I only want a couple of big trees in my yard. My dream house is two stories with a lot of small windows, but not too many windows. I don't want my house to be in a big neighborhood. I want my house to have a big garage that houses an all white, with black rims, Toyota Supra. My dream house would have a smooth brick driveway.

Dreams of a Purple House
By Char'Naja Moody (Grade 9)

My dream house is going to be in Miami. It's going to have four stories in the house. I'm going to have two dogs: a bulldog and a poodle. My house is going to be made out of glass and I want the trim around the glass to be purple. I'm going to have my own private property and three maids. Also, my house is going to be decorated by a designer. I want to live on Ocean Drive. There are going to be palm trees everywhere. My house is also going to be built by someone in my family. When I get old enough to be able to even get a house, I want to have 50 acres. I can't wait to pull my purple and silver Wrangler into my purple garage.

Dream House of Gold
By Jo'Shaun Palmer (Grade 9)

My dream house would be in the open with the sun shining and flowers dancing, with the grass green and cut smooth with no flaws. I would also have the biggest dogs protecting the front and the back of my house. The gold off of my house will reflect on the long-lasting driveway, making it look like the desert. Also, there will be sprinklers wetting the flowers so they grow.

I Hope
By Margaret (Big Margo) Pratt (Grade 12)

I hope for MMMh…
See, that's the thing
I don't know.
I don't want to hope,
'Cause having hope,
Isn't the same anymore.

I can't have hope,
Because I'm being always
Disappointed.

I had hope for a better
School year, and
Covid hit…
Another disappointment.

Having hope can get you so far.
I'm a senior and hope
Sometimes plays its part.

I don't think people should have hope.
I think it's more important to have heart.

I Believe
By Margaret (Big Margo) Pratt (Grade 12)

I need air.
I need space.
My anxiety is high.
My heart is at race.
Let me breathe.
Let me cry.

I don't know if
I'm gonna be alright.

May 6th,
Sleeping at night,
That night tore me to pieces:

4:00 AM
Woke to hear
You were no longer breathing.

Screaming inside.
Knowing no one could hear me.
Losing her made me prosper,
Because I'm knowing
She wanted better long days.

Stressful nights.
Can't sleep.
A long fight.
Knowing to believe.

But what I was believing wasn't right.
I felt abandoned.
No longer felt attached.
I believed it was ending.
I just didn't know believing
Is what really held me...

Dream House
By Avontae Ross (Grade 9)

My dream house is three story, with six rooms and beautiful green grass next to a smooth street, with a pool in the back of the house that has clear shining water. My house will have smooth white paint. I will have two dogs playing in the yard in the sun, while being protected by a gate.

Dream Home
By Deshawn Swanson (Grade 9)

My dream house is going to be a big, black house with like five dogs and a house phone and a lot of food and kids. I want a Sky Zone in my house with a basketball rim. And I want all my homeboys over and we going to play 2K. We going to have curry over my house and it's going to have a big gate. We going to play some Call of Duty. And then we going to play UFC and I'll have a lot of seafood and have a good time, and I really want a big tree by my house.

I Believe
By Asia Tillman (Grade 12)

I believe that everyone is in pain.
In my opinion, no one is truly happy.
Who enjoys waking up to a long day
Of school and work?
Who enjoys being hungry or sick?

Trauma
Your own family curse…
Who enjoys having only one parent
…or none at all?

Now, let me ask you this one question:
Who enjoys being alive?
Life has its beauty,
Don't get me wrong.
This planet has a pretty face.

But my time on this earth
Has not been very enjoyable,
But I am most grateful for the
Kind souls that I have
Let into my life.

Untitled
By Asia Tillman (Grade 12)

I hope for a mom and dad
To love me,
But it's too late.

I hope that one day
I will let down this way
I have between me and myself.

I hope to love and be friends with
Myself.

I hope for everyone to just
Love and be kind.

I hope for more,
But I don't wanna be greedy.

I hope for the sun, moon, and the stars.

I hope I'll one day become
One with earth and not with body
But with a soul.

I hope someday to be free.

Dream House
By Tiania Tyson (Grade 9)

My dream house would look like an all black house with red and white walls. The basement would have a basketball court inside, because I like to have a lot of company, so they can come over and hoop on my basketball court. Then I want to have a big game room with all the old NBA 2K games for my guests, and I want a built-in pool, so I wouldn't have to keep going to the beach to get inside of some cold water to cool off. I want to have a TV in my bathroom, so why you are using the bathroom, you could be entertained while you're using the bathroom. And I want to have a TV in the kitchen, so you can cook while watching your favorite show, or you could be watching a live basketball game while there. And I want to have a store outside my house, so people don't have to drive back and forth to the store, they could just go outside and there it is...convenient.

Dream House
By Javion Williams (Grade 9)

Three or four acres of back yard with a flower garden, go kart, basketball court, trees, a pond with lily pads so frogs play, a picnic sit-down spot, and a playground set for kids if I ever do have kids - this is my dream house. And in the front, I want a gate around my house and a front yard in-ground pool, with a couple trees, and two dogs that can play and be happy. Also, I want two cars: a G Wagon and McLaren in my garage.

I Believe

By Star Williams (Grade 12)

I believe that I can make a difference in this world.
I believe that we can make a difference in this city of
Benton Harbor, Michigan
With the ability to

PUT THE GUNS DOWN

And love one another...

I believe that there are other ways to handle situations.
I believe that if we want equal rights,
We can stop hurting each other and

FIGHT AS ONE

I believe the world will be at peace one day...

Chapter Eight
Thinking in Metaphor

I Am a Candle (Grade 12)
By Ta'Nae Allen

I am a candle,
I light up a room and glisten like stars,
dancing as I light up the sky.
Now you see the twinkling wonderful I bring as my
aroma fills the room with dreams,
dreams of being the star you see when you
feel at peace, as I sway across your consciousness.
I am your candle…

Namaste

I Am a Candle
By Marlon Bowman (Grade 12)

What do most people use a candle for?
Is it for my bright light or is it for the scent?
Now as much as a candle brightens up a dark room,
I brighten up someone's day.

I am the light in the dark for people when they have a bad day.
When I spread joy,
It is like when you blow out a scented candle.
Being someone's candle is not easy all the time,
Because I might not have enough stem to keep the room bright,
Which means I'm in a bad mood.

Hopefully, someone will be my candle in the dark someday, and
Will brighten my day.

A Rare Rose
By Aniya Daniels (Grade 12)

I'm a flower that's hard to come by;
Ready to flourish.
This might have not been my season,
But the next one will be.

Sometimes I wonder what it's like to be a cloud
Or even a leaf,
Floating wherever the wind takes me…

But then the sun reminds me
Why I am a Juliet Rose,
As it softly kisses my skin,
Because I was made to stand out.

Red Blanket
By Jordan Henry (Grade 12)

I am a red, cozy blanket,
warm and fuzzy,
but can become
too hot.

I am a grubby, red, blanket
that envelopes people,
and sometimes they feel smothered and
want to kick me away,
but sooner or later life can get cold and lonely,
and they start searching for me again
to engulf them with my warmth and comfort…

I Am a Mirror
By Paul Hicks III (Grade 12)

I am a mirror,
I can show you all types of things.
I can show you a magnificent makeover,
Or a horrible disfigurement.
I can show you your dazzling smile,
Or the monstrous chipped tooth you have.

I am a mirror,
I let you know when you look like a million dollars and two cents.
I can make your day or break it.

I am a mirror,
No matter what,
I will always tell you the truth.

I Am a Cell Phone
By Danny Jennings (Grade 12)

I am a cell phone—
The cause of human attachment and
Difficult to live without.
Please give me space,
I need some alone time.

I am a cell phone,
Forced to recharge for others' amusement.
Tired and abused,
Overheated and depleted.

I am a cell phone,
The keeper of many secrets hidden from the world,
With much responsibility;
I am the holder of restricted statistics.
I am a cell phone,
Tossed to the side at 1 am to recharge.
Cuddle me while you sleep.
I want to feel love.

I am a cell phone,
But I want to be a book.
Most people never misuse or abuse books.
They treasure them,
And learn from them.

Now I just need to find the most perfect library…

I Am a Roller Coaster
By Alexis Kirkland (Grade 12)

I am a rollercoaster.
My twists and turns
Leave you wondering
What I will do next.

I am a rollercoaster.
I am wild,
Going up and down
Without anyone expecting it.

I am a rollercoaster.
The thrill they get from being around me,
Whereas others find my
Height and speed scary.

I am a rollercoaster.
My wheels screech
To a sudden halt,
With the laughter of relief.

I Am a Seed
By Damarion Lewis (Grade 12)

I am a seed
That came in a pouch
To sprout into this world.
It might take a while for you to see me,
But I am changing slowly
Into something great.

I am a seed
That will succeed and grow
Up big and strong. I
Endure lots of water that
Keeps me hydrated and feeling as if
I'm on top of the world.

I am a seed
Who needs love and care
In order for me to sprout up to the
Tippy Top.

Seed Package Directions: We all come into this world from nothing, and over
time, with the right love and care, we can grow up to become something
extraordinary.

I Am a Football
By Tyler Meeks (Grade 12)

I am a football,
Soaring
Through the air,
Hoping
To be caught.
Being carried
With no known course.

I am a football,
The love for me changes lives,
Creating opportunities for students,
For those who need to create
A better future....

I Am a Tree
By Antonio Mendoza (Grade 9)

I am a tree,
Tall and strong,
That's sturdy and independent.

I am a tree,
I'll be there to stick around
When you need me,
But I can
Shake and violently when mad.

I am a tree that protects you
When being bothered by the sun on a hot day.
I am a tree everyone looks up to
And want to be as big as me.

I am a tree because
Because I'm hard to bring down.

I Am a Purse
By Char'Naja Moody (Grade 9)

I am a purple purse.
I am special and
Kept away from others;
I hold on to a lot of important things.

I am a purple purse,
One you can't afford...
I have silver, sparkle handles,
If I'm torn,
I will get upset.

I am a purple purse,
Something you can count on
To keep all your personal information
Safe and secure...

Imagine losing me…
What would you do?

I am a purple purse,
I get old with time.
I am a purple
Chanel bag

So you better cherish me!

I Am a Cloud
By Classie Newbern (Grade 12)

Clouds Clouds Clouds

Cumulus Cloud,
That's me.
I am very fun and versatile to be around and look at.
I seem to be very close to the world,
But it's an illusion,
In reality, I am very distant.

When you come across me,
I can become very bright and fluffy.
If you ever saw me,
You would just want to hold me and never let me go.
But don't get it twisted,
I, as well, have bad days too.
My anger can be very striking.
You will feel my dark energy when I am mad,
But just like clouds,
I too will eventually be bright and fluffy again.

As a cloud, I'm a good protector.
I'm always up and around for shade.
Whenever you need me,
Especially when you feel like you're gonna pass out,
I swiftly float
From out of the blue
To save you.
Whenever you need me, I'm always here.
Just looking at me could always lead to comfort,
Because you can always talk to me,

I am a cloud and the clouds are me...

I Am a Teddy Bear
By Davis Powell (Grade 12)

Teddy Bear

Why do you now want another snuggle?
Were you struggling?
I guess that it's hardly fair.
Then squeeze me away, I'm here every day.
You know I'll always be there.
You don't have to speak, just nuzzle my cheek.
If only you knew how to care…

Even so, we're small together, after all,
I'm only your Teddy Bear.
Even in the dark, I'm somehow your spark,
I'll drain you of worry and fear.

My shoulder is fine, with fabric aligned,
Invented for holding your tears.
Apart and by length, we must show our strength,
For our softness is all that we share.

I'll stay in this place, caressed by your grace—
And will always be your Teddy Bear.

Photo supplied by author

I Am a Broken Heart
By Kentrell Pullian (Grade 12)

I'm broken inside,
Like a broken heart.
No one cares about my feelings or how I'm living.
I have two sides of me,
Like a heart split in two. I have
Trust issues from how my past treated me.
I keep locking up
My heart
Because I know once I give it to someone,
They're going to take advantage of it,
And run with it—

I will never love again…

I Am Sunshine
By Avontae Ross (Grade 9)

I'm sunshine.
I can light up someone's day.
I can light up the darkest places.
I will always rise up.

I am sunshine.
I can be too warm,
So I try to dim down
To not blind you with my warmth…

I am sunshine.
I can help things grow and get more beautiful.
I can power things up, but
Sometimes the clouds block my light.

I am sunshine.
I give people my energy every day.
I help you see through the darkness.
Sometimes I can't be there,
But I will always be there behind the clouds,
Even if you can't see me.

I'm sunlight,
The most under-appreciated thing in the world.

I Am a Fan
By Kamerion Tillman (Grade 9)

I am a Fan,
Some days I am cold;
Some days I am hot,
Other days I don't work.

I can break.
I can be unplugged, and
Plugged up...

I have 3 different settings, low, medium, and high…
I am always changing,
Like the breeze…

Photo supplied by author

I Am a Cell Phone
By Tiania Tyson (Grade 9)

I am like a cell phone that can come to life if you want.
I can be used all day, but if I'm overused,
I will die -
But I can be recharged,
I will just need to sit for a bit…

I am a cell phone that can connect you to anything, and
Give you any direction.
I am a phone that has all your secrets,
And won't give them to anybody,
Unless I have your permission.

I am a cell phone that can't live without my spouse/owner.
I am a phone that needs apps to have a personality,
But I will need space

To breathe.

I am a phone.

If I break I can be repaired,
But it might cost a lot to get fixed,
Or you can get a new me,
But I won't have the same personality.

I need you to provide me with some protection.
I can be sad, be sad where sometimes
I don't want to charge,
Be sad where if I don't get texts or calls,
I can be on do not disturb.

I Am a Paint Palette
By Synesha Ware (Grade 12)

I am like a paint palette,
Flowing with colors of meaningful emotions.
The different shades of brown emerge
When the light shines on my skin.
The bold black matches the dark tone of my hair
Where the sunlight sinks in.
Vibrant and bright colors are my personality,
Shining like the sun's bright rays…
I am the brightest paint palette
That your eyes may see,
Shining bright and colorful,
Using all of the paints in my palette…

I Am a Camera
Jerome White Jr. (Grade 12)

I am like a camera with no filters.
You wish I had a filter so I could lie to you about
truths,
but I was programmed without a filter.
You can get mad and think what I am telling you is wrong,
but in truth,
what you see is something you have been
dreading for too long…
What you see is the true reflection of your inner self.
I am a camera with no filter.
Reality may hurt for a few moments,
but it's not my fault,
I can only tell the truth.

I Am a Cellular Device
By Kobe White (Grade 12)

I am a phone.
I am reliable.
I am intelligent.
You can depend on me.
I can be broken,
But still repair myself,
With help.
If I receive too much
Attention, my batteries
Die out.
I need to be alone
To recharge myself,
Before I can help others.

Lesson:
If we are identified with what we use and operate,
We will eventually merge with it and become it.

I Am a Fire!
By Star Williams (Grade 12)

I am a fire,
A pleasure to have around
In your darkest times;
A warmer for a cold soul.

I am a fire,
Someone to count on
To brighten things up.

I am a fire,
Calm at first,
But wild when fueled;
I'm hard to maintain
When you lose control of me.

If you are touched by me,
I'll leave a mark!
I am a fire,
Beware...

I am Headphones
By Damarious Woods (Grade 12)

I'm a beating and heartfelt little dragon

You can hear and see me

I'm headphones

I'm hard hitting and ruthless

I'm headphones

I'm joyful and heartbreaking

I'm headphones

I'm mad and angry

I'm headphones

I'm chained and unbreakable

I'm headphones

I'm controllable and unmatched

I'm headphones

Chapter Nine
Black and Orange

Being a Tiger Means to Me
By Ta'nae Allen (Grade 12)

Being a Tiger to me means having integrity. We are looked at as if we're less smart than any other school in Michigan, when we have so much to offer. Being a Tiger means to lead and not follow, because all eyes are on us. This school is all of us, as a community of Benton Harbor, have. There's nothing to tie us back together if we lost our school, so leading by example is the best start.

Tiger School Colors: Orange and Black
By Teonna Bell (Grade 12)

I believe that orange represents Benton Harbor High School, because for the time I have been attending, it has been sociable. BHHS gives happiness. The energy here is amazing. Everyone supports and looks out for each other. There is also enthusiasm now, which is why I believe orange represents Benton Harbor.

I think that black represents Benton Harbor High School; I believe this because the school shows strength. Benton Harbor High School is a big part of the community. The school is powerful and shows authority, just like the color black.

Being a Tiger Means to Me
By Kyle Booth (Grade 12)

Being a Tiger means to be brave, courageous, smart, and to have spirit. My freshman year it took me a long time to get used to the Tiger stuff. Once I started going to football games and basketball games, the energy of the community amazed me. It's one of a kind, and I love it.

Being a Tiger Means to Me
By Marlon Bowman (Grade 12)

Being a Tiger means to be a leader in this community. Also, it means stepping up and trying to make Benton Harbor a better place. To be a Tiger means you need to try to make the best choices in life to influence others too. I am a Tiger athlete and I hope to leave a legacy and set an example for the underclassmen. I think that is what it means to be a Tiger...legacy…

Being a Tiger Means to Me
By Mylon Bowman (Grade 12)

What a Tiger means to me is being a team, hard work, and commitment. Why? Because being a team as a Tiger shows help and love throughout the team. It shows that one is willing to work together to get things done for themselves, one another, and to help and love one another. Working hard as a Tiger shows that you really want it, and that no matter how hard things look, giving up is not an option. Being pushed to the limits to the very end is not a problem, but to keep moving forward with patience and hard work is the lesson. Having commitment as being a Tiger means not changing but staying as a tiger, that being a Benton Harbor Tiger is your home. Even if you move, but having a mentality that being a Tiger and having the commitment that you'll stay a Tiger will stay with you mentally, emotionally, and spiritually.

Being a Tiger Means to Me
By Emaria Campbell (Grade 12)

Being a Tiger means to me that we are competitive, self-confident, and brave. It also means you're powerful. So with that being said, you fight for what you believe in and what's right. Another thing is you never give up until you achieve what you are reaching for. That's what being a Tiger means to me.

Being a Tiger Means to Me
By Kenyatta Cooper (Grade 12)

Being a Tiger to me means everything. Everyone in my family graduated as a Tiger and I want to graduate as a Tiger too. Being a Tiger to me means that I will always strive to be my best self. As a school, we are overlooked and belittled. I feel if I do my best, I can prove otherwise. Being a Tiger to me means to never give up and to always have Tiger Pride.

Tiger School Colors: Orange and Black 12th
By Keewayn Fleming (Grade 12)

I believe the color orange represents Benton Harbor Tigers, because it is full of energy and so are the Tigers. Happiness represents Benton Harbor High school, because the students show their pride when at Benton Harbor High games. I believe enthusiasm is a part of Benton Harbor High School because its students are always eager to see the Benton Harbor Tigers Basketball team rule the court. I believe warmth represents Benton Harbor High School, because the color orange represents the warmth of the school. I believe the word security represents Benton High School, because the students and staff are secure when they enter the learning environment. Benton Harbor High School is a fun place to be.

I believe black represents our school, because strength represents Benton Harbor High School and the students at Benton Harbor High have great strength for learning. Mysterious is another word that can represent Benton Harbor High School because the students and staff excite curiosity. The color black represents elegance and so does Benton Harbor High School, because its students are sophisticated. Powerful represents Benton Harbor High school, because the athletes are strong and powerful at their games. When you enter through the doors of Benton Harbor High School, you will feel the joy of the building. Authority represents Benton Harbor High School, because the students are in charge of their learning environment.

Being a Tiger Means to Me
By William Fryson (Grade 12)

Being a Tiger means everything to me. Both of my parents were Tigers and graduated as Tigers. I've been through so much as a Tiger, and it's finally almost over. Being a Tiger means to go through tough times, but still come out strong.

Being a Tiger Means to Me
By Jordan Henry (Grade 12)

Being a Tiger means to me that we are very underrated and people always count us out. We are a strong group of people and have very strong support. The fact is my dad, mom, and my brother graduated from Benton Harbor High School. It makes me glad to be a Tiger, only because I would be the last out of my family to graduate from here. That's what being a Tiger means to me.

Being a Tiger Means to Me
By Danny Jennings (Grade 12)

If I'm being honest with you and me, I really don't know what it feels like being a Tiger. It's really confusing, because I repeatedly tried to think about what it means to me, but I never came up with an answer. I guess the feeling of being a Tiger just isn't in my blood. So, I apologize if I disappointed anyone with my lack of compassion.

Being a Tiger Means to Me
By Koreyanna Jones-Vison (Grade 12)

Being a Tiger means to be fierce, determined, ambitious, solitary, and to have courage. Fierce means to me to be powerful and a savage. To be determined means to set on or have a firm belief in something or someone. To have ambition means to me to have a strong desire or determination to do something. Solitary is by oneself, unaccompanied, lonely. Finally, the most important one: courage, which means bravery and the ability to do something you wouldn't normally do.

Tiger School Colors: Orange and Black
By Arlandrea Lamb (Grade 12)

I believe that orange represents Benton Harbor High School. Orange is warm, for example, when I first came to this school, all the teachers were very welcoming. Benton Harbor High School represents happiness, because it's a very supportive school, for example, prior to COVID, before games, we used to have pep rallies to get the boys prepared and ready for games. Lastly, Benton Harbor HS represents balance, because it's starting to become more organized, for example, we have in-person and virtual learning. We have learning choices to learn from home or at school. Our school thinks about the individual learning needs of the students, which many schools do not.

I believe that black represents Benton Harbor High School. Black is STRENGTH, for example, even though they wanted to shut our school down we fought to keep it open. BHHS represents powerful because as one we are a very strong group of individuals. Finally, Benton Harbor High School represents being mysterious, because I remember reading and it is a local legend that the third floor is haunted. For example, it was stated that shadows had been seen by janitors.

Being a Tiger Means to Me
By Jakira McClinton (Grade 12)

Being a Tiger to me is being strong and confident, no matter what outsiders think of Tigers. Being a Tiger to me being a leader who lots of people look up to at the high school. Being a Tiger to me represents that wherever I go, I represent Tigers. Being a Tiger to me is being a part of a big family. Being a Tiger to me is knowing my worth. Being a Tiger to me is loving myself.

Being a Tiger Means to Me
By Tyler Meeks (Grade 12)

Being a Tiger means to me that you are strong. Being from Benton Harbor is totally different from being from anywhere else. We have had to face so much adversity, from being threatened to being shut down and from violence to COVID-19. Being a Tiger means so much to me, because my parents didn't have the chance to be. They both were born and raised in Benton Harbor, but graduated from other schools. So now I have the chance to make a legacy and graduate as a Tiger.

Being a Tiger Means to Me
By Classie Newbern (Grade 12)

Being a Tiger means to me just never giving up on dreams and goals towards the future. I say that in the most humblest way possible, because from past situations, we have got dragged down from being a Tiger. Little do people know we are not called "Tigers" for nothing. We have powerful willpower with dedication and a lot of courage all in one. I'm proud to be called a Tiger, because being a tiger is a great thing, and we have and will continue to change the world with nothing but positivity, even when people have doubts. That's what I like about attending Benton Harbor High School, because it is not really as bad as people make it seem. It is just like judging a book by a cover, but instead of judging a book, it's judging a school you've never been to.

Being a Tiger Means to Me
By Davis Powell (Grade 12)

To be a Tiger means to aim for highest goals—more than the expected. We are overlooked, so we are willing to exceed what others expect from us, whether it's in class, sports, or the community, we will never cease to amaze. But we don't just do it for others' opinions, but for ourselves as well.

Being a Tiger Means to Me
By Kentrell Pullian (Grade 12)

Being a Tiger means to have a mentality of not giving up and focusing. Being a Tiger also means that we are different and have our own way of getting things done. It also means to be competitive, self-confident, and brave. We also take out our predators to survive and would do anything we need to get things done.

Tiger School Colors: Orange and Black 12th
By Jamarious Sanders (Grade 12)

The school I attend is named Benton Harbor High School. It is an energetic school. People here will welcome you with open arms and you will never get bored here, because teachers have a lot to teach you. You can arrive at school in the morning feeling bad, but you will leave here like you woke up with sunshine in your heart.

Along with our academics, extra-curricular activities are also organized at our school. This is one of the main reasons why I love my school, as it does not measure everyone on the same scale. Our hardworking staff gives time to each child to grow at their own pace, which instills confidence in them. My school has all the facilities of a library computer room, playground, basketball court, and more, to ensure we have it all at our disposal.

Some more cool facts about our school are our strengths. At one point in time, our school could have been shut down, but we didn't give up and we're still open. If someone asked me what I have learned from my school, I won't be able to answer it in one sentence. For the lessons are irreplaceable and I can never be thankful enough for them. I learned to share because of my school. The power of sharing and sympathy was taught to me by my school. I learned how to be considerate towards animals and it is also one of the main reasons why I adopted a pet.

Being a Tiger Means to Me
By Toney Walker (Grade 12)

Being a Tiger means to me taking responsibility for your actions, showing respect, and having a good attitude. Also, bringing the community together as one. And we are supposed to be civilized to one another. We also have some type of special faith to get through things.

Being a Tiger Means to Me
By Synesha Ware (Grade 12)

What it means to be a Tiger is to be outgoing and willing to work hard for what you got or want in life, and always being motivated and strong and being a great leader for everyone to see. Because being strong, motivated, outgoing, and willing to work hard
is why I'm the Tiger that I've become today.

What Being a Tiger Means to Me
By Kobe White (Grade 12)

Being a Tiger means to be resilient, because the people who reside here are very strong spirited. I have seen countless examples of "Tigers" who are the people who lift each other up, no matter what drought they are in, and no matter how many disbelievers are going against their will to fight for their home and their forest.

Do you know what thing allows me to consistently believe they're stronger spirited than most spirited communities? The fact that I'm from a town called Dowagiac, where their school spirit is nothing compared to the Benton Harbor Tigers. This just brings me to the conclusion that Tiger Pride is something that most people do not have.

I also believe that being a Tiger means having strength to fight the evil that lurks around Benton Harbor, no matter how much killings, debt, and police brutality can't keep a Tiger down forever. We always find a way to stand back up and finish our Business to move on to a bigger jungle.

I believe being a Tiger is fighting until you can't fight back anymore.

What Being a Tiger Means to Me
By Damarius Woods (Grade 12)

What it means to be a Benton Harbor Tiger is to never give up, even though the government wanted to shut us down, we never gave up and the school stayed open. We also have trust that the school will protect us when danger is near. We also trust the teachers, because they will be there for us when we need them the most.